# stitch it: quilts

16 quilted projects to make for your home

inspirations books

# contents

## recycled fabric

## tools & techniques

treasures

# lovely liquidambars

*This quilt is barely larger than a sheet of paper, making it a tiny treasure for your wall or table.*

Small quilts make wonderful artworks, with their beautiful fabrics and exquisitely neat stitching. Working in this size means that you can develop many different quilting and stitching techniques in complete projects. You can also use a wider variety of delicate fabrics, as a small art quilt will need less cleaning and not be subject to the same stresses and strains of use as a large quilt.

### materials and techniques

The tiny treasures on these pages are three variations on a theme. The basic leaf design (see page 132 for templates) is represented in three different quilting treatments.

The first quilt, pictured at left, comprises layers of gauzy fabric covered by free machine quilting stitches in white, red and gold. The effect of the rich texture and color is striking.

A second version of the quilt (see page 10) uses the basic leaf template in another form. The leaves in this quilt are a form of shadow work, with silky fabrics in glorious colors trapped beneath a very sheer silk gauze overlay. A series of lines of echo quilting are then stitched by hand through all of the layers.

The final version of the quilt (page 12) is a miniature wholecloth version. The leaf shapes are back stitched through all layers in contrasting primary colors, while the background areas are also hand quilted in a matching color to provide beautiful rippling texture on the white surface.

*Liquidambar leaves drift across this exquisite art quilt.*

# lovely liquidambars
## *machine quilting*

1

**materials**

*Scraps of beige silk, linen and cotton*

*One small long scrap of red silk*

*Artist's acrylic paint in gold*

*Soft paint brush*

*Liquidambar leaves*

*Gold, off-white and red machine sewing thread*

*10in x 16in (25cm x 40cm) cotton homespun*

*10in x 16in (25cm x 40cm) lightweight batting*

*Basic sewing equipment (see page 110)*

*Basic quilting equipment (see page 113)*

**step one**

Lay the homespun backing fabric right-side down on a flat surface, and place the batting on top. Lay strips of beige fabrics on top of the batting so that it is well covered with layers of fabric. Layer the strips horizontally to give an effect of layers of mist in an autumn forest.

Place the tapered piece of red silk last, on top of the other fabrics. Pin and baste all of the layers together.

*Finished size:*

*8in x 12in (20cm x 30cm)*

2

3

### step two

Thread the sewing machine with off-white thread and lower the feed dogs, according to the manufacturer's instructions. With the feed dogs lowered, stitch the layers of fabric in place using a long, straight stitch close to the raw edges of the strips of fabric.

Working on clean newspaper, paint the backs of the leaves, one at a time, with gold paint. Press the painted side of the leaf onto the quilt. Practice on scrap fabric. When the leaves have been printed onto the quilt, allow the paint to dry. Thread the sewing machine with gold thread. Lower the feed dogs and stitch around each of the leaf shapes as well as along some of the veins. Finish off all loose threads by pulling them through to the back of the quilt. Thread the ends into a needle and sew them into the homespun before cutting them off close to the fabric.

### step three

The quilting is done using a zigzag stitch and sewing with the feed dogs lowered. Work from side to side, spontaneously moving the quilt under the needle to create the illusion of mist. Use off-white thread for the majority of the quilt but use red over the red scrap of silk. It is nice to leave some areas of the quilt unstitched, although it is important to make sure that all frayed edges of the beige fabrics are covered.

Trim the edges of the quilt to a neat rectangle. Finish the edges with machine buttonhole or satin stitch. This is done with the feed dogs in the up position. Work right around the edges of the quilt once. Trim the edges of the quilt again if necessary, then restitch over the top of the first row of buttonhole stitch.

# lovely liquidambars
## shadow appliqué

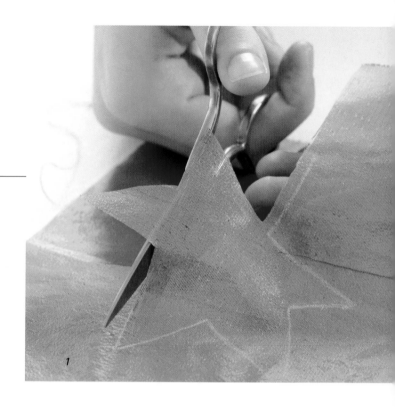

1

### materials

*10in x 16in (25cm x 40cm) beige silk dupion*

*10in x 16in (25cm x 40cm) beige homespun for
the backing*

*10in x 16in (25cm x 40cm) lightweight batting*

*10in x 16in (25cm x 40cm) white silk gauze*

*4in (10cm) squares of silk dupion – two hot pink,
two brown and one each of purple, mauve and
golden yellow*

*4in (10cm) beige homespun for the binding*

*Silk embroidery thread in colors to match the
silk leaves*

*Gütermann beige quilting thread*

*Crewel needle, no. 9; betweens needle, no. 9*

*Basic sewing equipment (see page 110)*

*Basic quilting equipment (see page 113)*

**Finished size:**

**8in x 12in (20cm x 30cm)**

### step one

Make a tracing of the leaf pattern from page 132
and use it to cut out each of the seven liquidambar
leaves from the squares of coloured silk dupion. Cut
two leaves each from the hot pink and brown pieces.
Cut one leaf from each of the other colours.

Try to avoid allowing the edges of the leaves to fray,
although one of the charms of the work is the small
amount of fraying that will inevitably occur.

Lay the homespun right-side down on a flat surface,
then lay the batting and the beige silk dupion
right-side up on top. Using the layout diagram on
page 132, place the leaves on top of the quilt.
Carefully lay the silk gauze over the top of the leaves.
Pin and baste through all the layers, making sure that
the leaves do not move.

2

3

### step two

Back stitch around each leaf through all of the layers of
the quilt, using a single strand of matching silk thread
and the crewel needle. Back stitch along the veins of the
leaves with the same thread.

When all of the leaves have been outlined and the veins
stitched, begin hand quilting. Using Gütermann beige
quilting thread and the betweens needle, start stitching
around the leaves, making sure that the work lies flat as
you stitch.

The quilting stitches should be ⅛in (3mm) long and the
rows should be ⅛in (3mm) apart.

### step three

When all the stitching is complete, place the work on
the ironing board with the right side down. Hover the
steam iron over the reverse side of the quilt and allow
the steam to flatten it out. Do not press the iron onto
the quilt. Allow the quilt to cool before moving it. Trim
the edges to make a neat rectangle, if necessary.
Cut strips of the homespun fabric for the binding
1¼in (3cm) wide across the width of the fabric. Join
the strips together to make a single strip measuring
60in (140cm) long. Press the strip in half lengthwise
and stitch it to the outer edges of the quilt, mitring
the corners as you go. See page 125 for detailed
instructions on binding a quilt and mitring the corners.

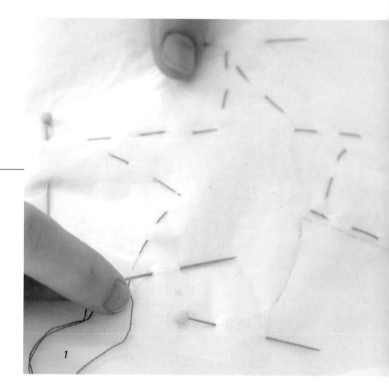

# lovely liquidambars
*hand quilted*

## materials

*Three pieces of white homespun, each 10in x 16in*
*(25cm x 40cm)*
*4in (10cm) white homespun for the binding*
*Stranded embroidery cotton in white, dark brown,*
*mid brown, light brown red, blue, gold and*
*olive green*
*Crewel needle, no. 9*
*Soft tracing paper and pencil*
*Basic sewing equipment (see page 110)*
*Basic quilting equipment (see page 113)*

**Finished size:**
**8in x 12in (20cm x 30cm)**

1

### step one

Place the three layers of homespun on top of one another. With homespun, there is no real right side, but if you are using fabric with a definite right and wrong side, make sure that the right sides of the top and bottom layers are facing outwards. The middle layer of fabric in this quilt takes the place of batting. Trace the leaf template from page 132 onto soft tracing paper, following the layout design. Place the tracing paper on top of the layers of cloth and pin it in place. (Note that our sample shows only one leaf for clarity. You should trace all of the leaves of the pattern at once.) Baste around each of the leaves through all of the layers. Baste around the edges of the quilt.

2

3

## step two

When the basting is complete, tear away the paper pattern. Back stitch each of the leaves using two strands of embroidery cotton and a crewel needle. Working from left to right, stitch the leaves in dark brown, gold, mid brown, blue, red, light brown and olive green. Stitch the leaf veins in back stitch in the same colour as the outlines.

When the back stitching of the leaves is complete, hand quilt with a running stitch around each of the leaf shapes, using two strands of white embroidery cotton and a crewel needle. Echo quilt in the spaces around the leaves, making sure that the work lies flat as you stitch. (See page 123 for more details on hand quilting.)

## step three

When all the stitching is complete, place the quilt with the right-side down on an ironing board and hover a steam iron over the back. Do not press the iron into the quilt. Allow the quilt to cool before moving it. Trim the edges to make a neat rectangle, if necessary. Cut strips of the fabric for the binding 1¼in (3cm) wide across the width of the fabric. Join the strips together to make a single strip measuring 60in (140cm) long. Press the strip in half lengthwise and stitch it to the outer edges of the quilt, mitring the corners as you go. See page 125 for detailed instructions on binding a quilt and mitring corners.

# bling-bling bolero

*Crazy patchwork and embroidery adds zing to
a simple bolero-style vest.*

Quilted clothing is part of a long historical tradition. When human beings first began to clothe themselves, they layered animal skins together with dried grasses and stitched them with bone needles and sinew. Later, woven fabrics and felt replaced animal skins but the technique of layering for warmth and strength continued.
Being human, it was not long before the stitching and fabrics became decorative as well as functional: sometimes the patterns represented the natural world and sometimes they were included as mystical symbols. These days, with technology able to provide warmer and stronger garments and different ways to fuse the layers together, quilted clothing is less of a necessity. Beautiful patchwork and exquisite stitching makes quilted clothing a true work of art rather than a functional item.

### materials and techniques

The bolero shape is a simple design that is flattering for many figure types. This version of the bolero is decorated with crazy patchwork panels in silks, satins and taffetas. An overlay of sheer, shimmering organza is quilted and embroidered to give a rich, jewel-like finish.

*Add some art to your wardrobe with a wearable quilt. The quilt on the bed is the Cherry Pie quilt on page 20.*

# bling-bling bolero

1

## materials

Commercial bolero pattern (with no darts)

Quantity specified by pattern of lightweight
quilt batting

Quantity specified by pattern of black silk fabric

Quantity specified by pattern of black satin
lining fabric

Selection of silk, satin and taffeta fabric scraps in
jewel colors

40in (1m) white or pale silver organza

3½yd (3m) organza ribbon, ⅝in (1.5cm) wide

Silver metallic embroidery thread

Selection of fancy embroidery threads and yarns
to coordinate with fabrics

³/₁₆in (4mm) round sequins to coordinate
with fabrics

1oz (50g) seed beads to coordinate with fabrics

Black machine sewing or quilting thread

Basic sewing equipment (see page 110)

Basic quilting equipment (see page 113)

## step one

Pin the commercial bolero pattern pieces to the
lightweight quilt batting. Cut out the shapes from the
batting. Referring to the photographs of the bolero
on page 19, mark out the areas of the vest front and
back that you will cover with crazy patchwork.
Apply small, irregular shaped pieces of silk, satin and
taffeta fabric to the lightweight quilt batting. Begin
by cutting a four- or five-sided shape and placing it
roughly in the centre of the area to be covered by
patchwork. Pin it in place. Take the next piece of
fabric and lay it on top of the first piece with right
sides together. Align one straight edge of each piece
of fabric. Pin, and stitch along the aligned edge. Turn
the fabric over and press the seam flat.

2

3

### step two

Continue to add pieces of fabric in the same way until the entire area is covered. You may need to appliqué some shapes in place to ensure that no raw edges are visible. Simply press a seam allowance under on the piece of fabric you want to appliqué, then you can either slip stitch it in place or machine stitch it close to the pressed edge. See page 117 for more information on piecing crazy patchwork.

Completely cover the marked areas with crazy patchwork. Allow the raw edges of the outer pieces of silk, satin and taffeta fabric to remain unfinished, as you will later cover them with black satin fabric.

### step three

Begin laying fancy embroidery threads and yarns over the crazy patchwork in swirls and curved lines. Lay the threads in a diagonal direction across the bolero pieces, but don't be too concerned about keeping the lines parallel. Use black sewing thread or thread of a matching color to couch the yarns and threads in place. Couching is simply using small, straight stitches at regular intervals to hold the decorative threads in place on the surface of the fabric. See page 128 for stitching instructions.

### step four

Cut out pieces of organza to cover the crazy patchwork
sections of the bolero. Pin the organza in place and use
long running stitches to baste it down. Stitch across
the organza fabric so that it won't move during the
following stages of embellishing and sewing the bolero.
Cut black satin fabric to cover the exposed areas of
the lightweight batting, including a 5/8in (1.5cm) seam
allowance on all sides. Press the seam allowance under
on the edges of the satin that will overlap the crazy
patchwork areas. Use long running stitches to baste
the black fabric in place.

### step five

Using black machine quilting thread, machine stitch
along the edge of the black satin fabric, close to the
pressed fold. Stitch three lines of quilting 1¼in (3cm)
apart, echoing the curve at the edge of the black
fabric. We have used contrasting quilting thread in the
photograph for clarity; however, you should use black
thread on the black silk fabric.

Using metallic embroidery thread, embellish the
organza-covered crazy patchwork with feather stitch
worked in the spaces between the couched yarns and
threads. See page 129 for instructions on working
feather stitch.

### step six

Add sequins and seed beads to accent the feather stitching and couched thread patterns, as shown in the photograph above. Cut pieces of organza ribbon each three times longer than the seams that join the black fabric and the crazy patchwork. Stitch along the ribbon with long running stitches, beginning with a secure knot and working in a zigzag pattern along the length of the ribbon. Red thread has been used in the photograph for clarity; however, you are advised to use black thread to match the ribbon.

Pin one end of the ribbon to the edge of the bolero piece, then gather the ribbon by holding the other end of the running stitch thread and drawing up the ribbon until it fits the seam. Tie off the end of the running stitch thread close to the gathered ribbon to hold the ruching in place. Pin the ruched ribbon around the curve of the seam and hand stitch it in place, adding seed beads as you go. Remove any remaining tacking stitches and make up the bolero according to the directions given in the commercial pattern.

# cherry pie quilt

*This queen-size, foundation-pieced quilt will
surely be treasured as a family heirloom.*

A large, double or queen-size quilt like the one on these pages is
quite an undertaking, but the effort that you put into making it will
be amply repaid by the accolades you will receive from your family
and friends. This quilt, with its exquisite foundation-pieced sawtooth
blocks and appliqué of cherry blossoms and blackbirds, was originally
designed and made as a wedding present. In many years' time, the
children and grandchildren of the happy couple will still appreciate the
skill and dedication of the quilter.

## materials and techniques

This style of quilt is called a medallion quilt because the structure of
the quilt is a series of symmetrical borders around a central motif, or
medallion. The central motif of this quilt was inspired by a design by
Janet Miller, in her book *At the Heart of Folkart* (The City Stitcher,
2000). The borders are constructed from 7in (18cm) sawtooth blocks
and 7in (18cm) pieced blocks set on point. Foundation piecing ensures
precise points and an exact finished size of each segment, which
is essential when there is no room for error. An appliqué of cherry
branches ties the borders to the central motif.

*Turn the master
bedroom into a snug
retreat with this
masterful application
of the quilting arts.*

# cherry pie quilt

## materials

*240in (6m) cream cotton fabric for medallion*
*background and pieced borders*
*40in (1m) tan cotton fabric for pieced arrow blocks*
*80in (2m) olive green cotton fabric for leaves, stems*
*and binding*
*80in (2m) mid green cotton fabric for inside border*
*120in (3m) deep green cotton fabric for outside border*
*Nine fat quarters of colored cotton print fabrics for*
*pieced blocks and small appliqué pieces*
*Six fat eighths of red cotton print fabrics for cherries*
*One fat eighth of dark brown cotton fabric for*
*blackbird appliqué*
*8yd 18in x 44in (7.5m x 115cm) fabric for quilt backing*
*90in x 100in (230cm x 260cm) medium weight batting*
*Freezer paper*
*Sewing thread to match appliqué fabrics*
*Stranded embroidery cotton in mid green to match*
*fabric and black*
*Template plastic*
*Thin card*
*Thin paper (such as scrapbook paper)*
*Dressmaker's carbon paper (optional)*
*Tweezers*
*Basic sewing equipment (see page 110)*
*Basic quilting equipment (see page 113)*

**Finished size: 90in x 100in (228.5cm x 255cm)**

## step one

Prewash all fabric to prevent shrinkage after the quilt
is assembled. Prepare the templates and patterns from
pages 133–6 as follows. Enlarge and trace the shapes
for the bird, leaves and the other elements of the
appliqué (there is no need to make templates for the
stems) onto template plastic. Cut out circles of thin
cardboard for the cherries: use a small coin such as a
nickel or a five cent piece as a guide.

Prepare master copies of the patterns for foundation
piecing (see pages 134–5). Trace the patterns onto
plain paper and work only from these master copies
from now on.

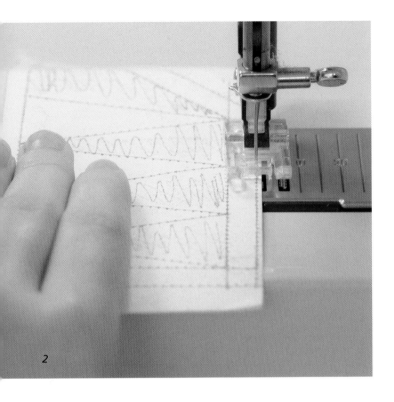

2

## step two

Using the master copy, trace or photocopy 72 copies each of patterns A and B for the pieced blocks. Using the master copy, trace or photocopy 66 copies each of patterns C and D for the sawtooth border blocks. Try this quick method: place a photocopy of the master copy on top of six to eight sheets of thin paper (use the pages from inexpensive scrapbooks, for example) and secure them together with paper clips. Using an unthreaded sewing machine (and an old needle), sew along all the lines on each pattern, as well as the outside cutting line.

Trace pattern E four times onto a sheet of paper for the outside border corners.

## step three

Before you begin cutting, set aside 12 ziplock plastic bags or small plastic containers. As you cut each set of different sized pieces, especially the triangles, place them in a separate bag with a label for easy identification later.

Cut a 20½in x 30½in (52cm x 77.5cm) piece of cream fabric for the centre appliqué panel. Cut two strips of cream fabric 5½in x 70⅞in (14cm x 180cm), and two strips of cream fabric 5½in x 80⅞in (14cm x 2m). These strips will form the background for the cherry appliqué border.

From the cream fabric, cut 17 squares measuring 11¼in (28.5cm). Cut each of these squares across both diagonals to yield four triangles. Label these "triangle one": you will use 66 of them for the borders. Cut two squares measuring 5⅞in (14.75cm). Cut each of these squares once diagonally to yield a total of four triangles. Label these "triangle two": they will be used for the outer border corners.

From the olive green fabric, use the leaf template to cut out 90 leaves, allowing a ¼in (6mm) seam allowance around each shape. From the same fabric, cut bias strips 1in (2.5cm) wide. (See page 115 for instructions on cutting on the bias.) You will need fifty-two 7in (18cm) lengths for the stems in the appliqué border, as well as two 7in (18cm) lengths and two 13in (32.5cm) lengths for the central appliqué design.

Also from the olive green fabric, cut nine strips 3½in (9cm) wide across the width of the fabric for the binding. From the mid green fabric, cut seven squares measuring 11¼in (28.5cm) for the inner border. Cut each of these squares across both diagonals to yield four triangles. Label these "triangle three". From the same fabric, cut eight squares measuring 5⅞in (14.75cm). Cut each of these squares once diagonally to yield a total of 16 triangles. Label these "triangle four". Lastly, cut nine squares measuring 5⅝in (14.5cm). Cut each of these squares across both diagonals to yield four triangles, for a total of 36 triangles. Label these "triangle five".

From the deep green fabric for the outer border, cut eight squares measuring 5⅝in (14.5cm). Cut each of these squares across both diagonals to yield four triangles. Label these "triangle six": you will use 30 of them for the outer border. From the same fabric, cut two 3in (7.5cm) squares. Cut each of these squares once diagonally to yield a total of four triangles. Label these "triangle seven".

From the deep green fabric, cut two 5½in (14cm) wide strips, each 90⅞in (230cm) long. Cut two 5½in (14cm) wide strips, each 100⅞in (256cm) long. These strips will make up the outer border of the quilt top.

From the fat eighths of red fabric, use the cherry template to trace 26 cherries from each colour fabric, adding a ¼in (6mm) hem allowance around the shape. You should have a total of 156 cherries.

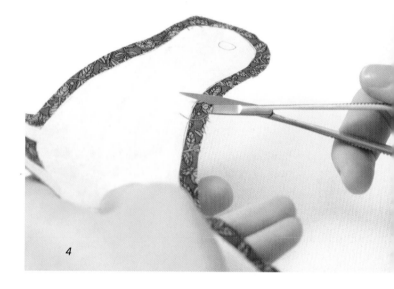

4

### step four

Fold the background fabric for the center panel in half horizontally and vertically, and press the creases. Using dressmaker's carbon paper or your preferred method, transfer the appliqué design from page 133 onto the center of the panel. Use the templates you made in step one for the birds and other appliqué pieces to cut the shapes from freezer paper. This can then be ironed onto the right side of the fabrics to provide a guide.

Cut out the shapes around the freezer paper, leaving a ¼in (6mm) hem allowance around the outline. Clip the curved edges of the fabric up to the edge of the paper and press the hem to the wrong side of the shape.

5

6

### step five

Take the olive green bias strips for the appliqué and fold the raw edges towards the center of the strip to make a strip ³⁄₈in (1cm) wide. Be careful not to stretch the edges of the strips at this stage. Use a bias bar, if you have one, to make this job easier. Press the strip and turn it over so the raw edges are underneath. Place the bias strips and other appliqué shapes on the background fabric, gently stretching the bias strips around the curves. Pin and baste the shapes in place. Using a thread to match the fabric, work needleturn appliqué around the edges of the shapes. See page 121 for instructions on needleturn appliqué. Remove the freezer paper when you have finished stitching.

### step six

Using thread to match the fabrics, sew a running stitch around the middle of the seam allowance of the cherry pieces. Place a circle of thin cardboard (see step one) on the wrong side of the fabric and gather the running stitches. Press the cherries with a hot iron to create a firm edge. Remove the cardboard before stitching the cherries to the background fabric. It might help to wet the card slightly to soften it.

Appliqué the cherries in place on the background fabric. Use three strands of green stranded cotton to work the cherry stems in stem stitch. Use two strands of black stranded cotton to work the birds' eyes and beaks in satin stitch. See page 131 for instructions on working these stitches.

### step seven

Make 18 pieced arrow blocks for the first border. Each block measures 7in (18cm). Make two blocks using each of the nine fat quarter fabrics, combined with the tan background fabric. Use the paper patterns marked A and B that you copied from page 135: you will need four each of both A and B for each block.

Lay a piece of tan background fabric right-side up on top of one of the paper pattern pieces, covering the area marked 1. Make sure the fabric extends at least ¼in (6mm) over the stitching lines and beyond the cutting lines of the pattern.

Position a piece of colored fabric with right-side down over the tan piece, so that the seam allowances align. Make sure the second fabric will extend at least ¼in (6mm) over the stitching lines and beyond the cutting lines of the pattern section marked 2, when it is turned over. Turn the pattern over and pin the fabric layers to the paper pattern. Place the pattern and fabric paper-side up in the sewing machine, which should be threaded with thread to match the quilt fabrics. Stitch along the line on the paper pattern, using a short stitch. Fold the paper pattern back along the sewn line, and trim the seam allowance to exactly ¼in (6mm). Unfold the paper and open out the second piece of fabric so that the seam sits flat. Press the seam. Add another piece of tan background fabric (piece 3). Make sure the fabric extends at least ¼in (6mm) over the stitching lines and beyond the cutting lines of the pattern section marked 3. Stitch as before. Continue adding alternate pieces of tan and colored fabric in the numbered order until you have completely covered the paper pattern. Press with an iron then trim with a rotary cutter along the outside punctured line. Leave the paper in place until the quilt top is completely assembled, then tear away the paper and press the seams flat again.

## step eight

Use the paper patterns marked C and D from page 135 (see step one). You will need 36 blocks each of pattern C and D.

Lay a piece of cream background fabric right-side up on top of one of the paper pattern pieces marked C, covering the area marked 1. Make sure the fabric extends at least ¼in (6mm) over the stitching lines and beyond the cutting lines of the pattern.

Position a piece of green border fabric over the cream piece with right sides together, so that the seam allowances align. Make sure the second fabric extends at least ¼in (6mm) over the stitching lines and beyond the cutting lines of the pattern section marked 2. Turn the pattern over and pin the fabric layers to the paper pattern. Place the pattern and fabric paper-side up in the sewing machine, which should be threaded with thread to match the quilt fabrics. Stitch along the line on the paper pattern, using a short stitch length.

Fold the paper pattern back along the sewn line, and trim the seam allowance to exactly ¼in (6mm). Unfold the paper and open out the second piece of fabric so that the seam sits flat. Add another piece of green border fabric (piece 3). Make sure the fabric extends at least ¼in (6mm) over the stitching lines and beyond the cutting lines of the pattern section marked 3. Stitch as before. Continue adding alternate pieces of cream and green fabric in the numbered order until you have completely covered the pattern. Press with an iron then trim with a rotary cutter along the outside punctured line. Leave the paper in place until the quilt top is completely assembled, then tear away the paper and press the seams flat again.

You will also need to complete four pieces of the pattern marked E (page 134) for the corners of the outer sawtooth border.

*8*

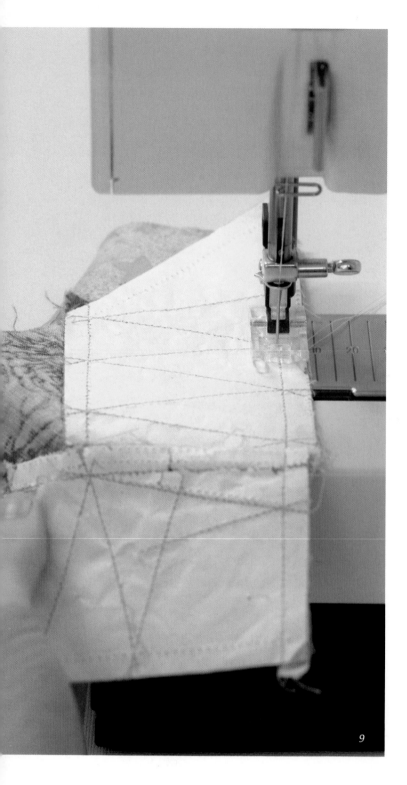

9

### step nine

Sew a pieced and trimmed pattern D block to one of the shorter sides of a "triangle five", matching seam allowances. Sew a pieced and trimmed pattern C block to the opposite short side of the triangle and across the end of the pattern D block. Continue until all of the sawtooth C and D blocks have been attached to "triangle five"s, to create sawtooth triangles.

Join a sawtooth triangle to a "triangle one", along one of the shorter edges so that the longer edges of the two triangles are parallel when they are opened out. Join another sawtooth triangle to the remaining short edge of the "triangle one", then join another "triangle one" to the remaining short edge of the sawtooth triangle. Continue until you have a strip of four sawtooth triangles alternating with three "triangle one"s. Refer to the quilt diagram on page 22 for details. Create a second strip in the same manner. Attach these two strips to the side edges of the appliqué background fabric with the cream "triangle one"s closest to the appliqué.

Join three sawtooth triangles alternating with two "triangle one"s. Make a second strip in the same manner. Join these two strips to the upper and lower edges of the appliqué panel with the cream "triangle one"s closest to the appliqué.

Carefully fold the corners so that the raw edges of the outer triangles of each border strip meet. Pin and stitch a ¼in (6mm) seam along the angled edge to complete the border with mitred corners.

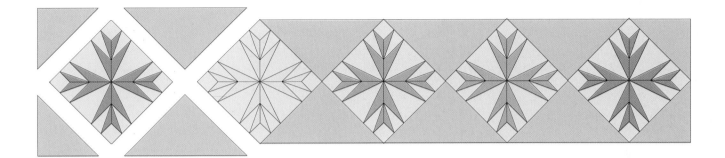

### step ten

For the pieced block border, alternate pieced arrow blocks with pairs of "triangle three", joining the short sides of the triangles to the arrow blocks so that they are set on point. Sew two strips, each comprising four pieced blocks joined together on point with three pairs of green "triangle three"s. At each end of the strip, add two "triangle four" pieces, attaching the longer edges of the "triangle four"s to the sides of the pieced block to finish the rectangular strip with a flat end. Attach these strips to the side edges of the quilt top.

Make two more strips of pieced blocks in the same manner, alternating five pieced blocks with pairs of "triangle three". Finish the strips with two "triangle four" pieces at each end as before. Attach these two strips to the upper and lower edges of the quilt top to complete the pieced block border.

### step eleven

Refer to step nine and create two sawtooth border strips, each alternating six sawtooth triangles with seven triangle one pieces. Attach the completed strips to the side edges of the quilt top with the sawtooth triangles closest to the pieced block border. See the diagram on page 22 for details.

Create two more sawtooth border strips, each using five sawtooth triangles and seven "triangle one" pieces. Attach the completed strips to the upper and lower edges of the quilt top with the sawtooth triangles closest to the pieced block border.

Carefully fold and stitch the mitred corners as in step nine, to complete the border.

12

### step twelve

Take the strips of cream fabric cut for the appliqué border (see step two) and fold them in half across the short axis to mark the middle by finger pressing. Fold and finger press the quilt top in half horizontally and vertically to mark the middle of each edge. Lining up the middle of the 80$\frac{7}{8}$in (2m) strips with the middle of the side edges of the quilt top, stitch the strips to the side edges. There will be excess fabric at either end of the border.

Lining up the middle of the 70$\frac{7}{8}$in (180cm) strips with the middle of the upper and lower edges of the quilt top, stitch these strips to the remaining edges. Leave the excess fabric at each end unstitched.

Carefully fold the quilt top diagonally so that the excess fabric strips at the corners are aligned with right sides together. Using the mitred corner of the sawtooth border as a guide, stitch a seam at a 45 degree angle from the edge of the sawtooth border to the outer edge of the strips to create a mitred corner. Check that the border sits flat, then trim the seam allowance to ¼in (6mm).

### step thirteen

Create the outer sawtooth border by alternating eight sawtooth triangles with seven trangle one pieces. Attach a "triangle two" piece at each end of the strip. Make two of these strips and attach them to the side edges of the quilt top with the cream triangles closest to the cream border fabric.

For the upper and lower borders, assemble seven sawtooth triangles alternating with six "triangle one" pieces. Take the pieced pattern E blocks and attach a "triangle seven" piece to the shorter side of the E block. Sew one of these to each end of the sawtooth border strips. Attach the strips to the upper and lower edges of the quilt top.

Refer to step twelve and mark the middle of each edge of the quilt top as well as the middle of the deep green border strips by finger pressing. Attach the two longer strips to the side edges of the quilt top, leaving the excess fabric at the ends as for the appliqué border background. Attach the two remaining strips of deep green fabric to the upper and lower edges. Mitre the corners as in step twelve.

### step fourteen

Using dressmaker's carbon paper, or your preferred method, transfer the cherry border appliqué design onto the background strip border. Refer to the photograph at left for placement. Appliqué the bias strips for the stems. Next appliqué the leaves and the cherries, then stem stitch the cherry stems using three strands of green stranded cotton.

Now the quilt top is complete, tear off the paper used in the foundation piecing. Tweezers can help you get rid of the hard-to-remove pieces. Carefully press the quilt top from the back.

Cut the backing fabric into three 2.5m (98in) lengths, remove selvedges and join the lengths together along the side edges. Press the seams flat. This will give a single piece of backing fabric large enough for the quilt. On a flat surface, lay this backing piece right-side down. Lay down the batting and the quilt top, right-side up. Baste the layers together and quilt by hand or machine according to your preference. The quilt shown on these pages was professionally machine quilted. Trim off excess backing fabric and batting. See page 122 for instructions on making a quilt sandwich, basting and quilting.

Join the strips of binding fabric into one long strip. Fold in half lengthwise with right side out and press. With the raw edges of the binding strip aligned with the raw edges of the quilt, stitch all the way around the edge, mitring the corners as you go. See page 125–7 for instructions on binding and mitring corners. Join the ends of the strip by tucking one inside the other and turning over a small hem on the outer end.

Fold the binding over to the back of the quilt and slip stitch the folded edge to the stitching line.

decorating your home

# Victorian virtuoso

*Crisp, white fabric, quilted and hand colored,
makes a stunning wall quilt.*

The pretty blue-and-white designs of Delft tiles come to mind with this beautiful monochrome quilt. Inspired by an etched glass design, the elaborate quilting pattern has a modern effect while recalling some of the antique beauties of the art nouveau era. Swarovski crystals accent the quilting.

### materials and techniques

The color on this quilt is applied by a new technique known as Colourque®. Using colored pencils, you color in the design directly on the fabric of the quilt, just as you did in your childhood coloring books. After applying a sealer to blend and fix the color, you quilt around the design to finish the quilt. It's so easy, and gives a fantastic effect.

*This pristine blue and white quilt gives a clean, modern effect.*

# Victorian virtuoso

**materials**

*2yd 31in (2.6m) good quality white cotton fabric,*
*prewashed and pressed*

*52in (130cm) square of quilt batting*

*Derwent Coloursoft pencils in #C290 Ultramarine,*
*#C370 Pale Blue*

*Metal pencil sharpener*

*Textile medium*

*Small round or flat paintbrush*

*600 grit wet-and-dry silicon paper*

*White sewing cotton*

*Aurifil cotton quilting thread #1128, 28 and 40 weight*

*500 Swarovski 2mm hot fix crystals in sapphire, plus*
*applicator wand*

*2B pencil or tailor's chalk*

*Sandpaper board (optional)*

*Basic sewing equipment (see page 110)*

*Basic quilting equipment (see page 113)*

*Finished size:*

*36⅝in x 41⅜in (93cm x 105cm)*

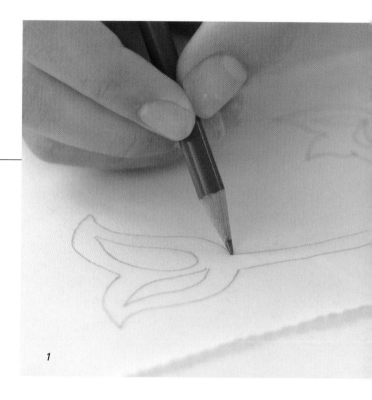

1

**step one**

From the white fabric, cut four 2½in (5cm) strips across the width of the fabric and set them aside for the binding. Cut the remainder into two pieces each measuring 48in (122cm). Set one of the pieces aside to use for the quilt back and work with the quilt top only. Use the leftover fabric to practice your coloring technique.

Fold the quilt top in half and finger press the fold. Use a needle and contrasting thread to stitch a running stitch along the crease. Repeat this in the opposite direction, dividing the quilt into quarters.

Enlarge the quarter pattern from page 137. Use a light box or tape the pattern and fabric to a sunlit window. Placing the center of the pattern in the center corner of one quarter of the quilt top. Trace all of the lines onto the fabric. Repeat for each quarter.

### step two

The following two steps describe the Colourque® technique developed by the designer of this quilt, Helen Stubbings.

Work on a hard, smooth surface. A kitchen counter or a glass table top are suitable, or you could make yourself a coloring board from medium density fibreboard (MDF). Place the 600-grit silicon paper under the area of fabric you wish to colour. The silicon paper acts as a stabilizer for the fabric and also helps to take the colour from the pencil onto the fabric. You need to keep your pencils sharp with a good quality metal pencil sharpener.

Derwent Coloursoft pencils (made by the Cumberland Pencil Company in the United Kingdom) have a very soft color shaft and behave a little bit like watercolor pencils. They come in a range of 72 colors.

Work on small parts of the design, coloring an area, then sealing it and leaving it to dry (see step three). You can work on another part of the quilt top while an area is drying.

Using #C370 (Pale Blue), color the design in a solid color. Color quite darkly and evenly, taking the color right up to the outline. Using #C290 (Ultramarine) with a very sharp point, add definition to the curves. Add a little of this color at the points of the shapes, and along one edge of long, curvy shapes. Use fine feathery strokes, flicking the pencil from the outline inwards. Make the lines in varied lengths so as not to get a definite line between the two shades. However, don't be too concerned if your blending is not perfect, as the application of the textile medium sealer will help to blend the colours further.

3

### step three

Once you have finished coloring a section of the design you need to seal it. Place a small amount of textile medium onto a palette, a tile or plate. Using a small paintbrush, lightly dab the textile medium onto the colored areas and paint over it carefully. Because the pencil behaves a little like a watercolor pencil, the brush and medium will 'move' the color.

Use the textile medium to blend and smooth your pencil coloring. Be careful not to get any of the textile medium onto the background fabric outside the lines, as it will stain. When you have a good coverage of textile medium on the colored area, leave that section of the quilt for at least half an hour to dry.

Repeat the Colourque® process until you have completed coloring the entire design. This will take you many hours, so take your time and aim for a two- to three-hour session for each section of the design.

The sealing process will prevent 'crocking' of your color and prevent it from rubbing or wearing off. Crocking is the movement of colour from one area of the quilt to another.

## step four

When the entire colored design is finished, sealed
and dry, prepare the quilt sandwich. See page 122
for detailed instructions.

Press both the colored top and the backing fabric
piece (see step one) well. Lay the backing fabric
right-side down on a table or a clean floor. Smooth
the batting over the top and center the quilt
top right-side up on top of that. Trim any excess
batting back to approximately 2in (5cm) from
the edges of the quilt top. Excess fabric will be
trimmed off in step five.

Pin all of the layers together and baste right across
the quilt in a 2in (5cm) grid pattern.

For the machine quilting, use the 28-weight Aurifil
thread in the top of your sewing machine and the
40-weight thread in the bobbin. Lower the feed
dogs (read the manufacturer's instructions for your
sewing machine if you don't know how to do this).
For best results, use a darning or quilting foot.
Begin slowly and steadily to outline quilt all
coloured areas of your design. Be careful to keep
smooth curves and sharp points where they are
needed. You may need to practice on some scraps
of fabric and batting first to check your tension
and the speed at which you move your quilt to get
a consistent stitch length.

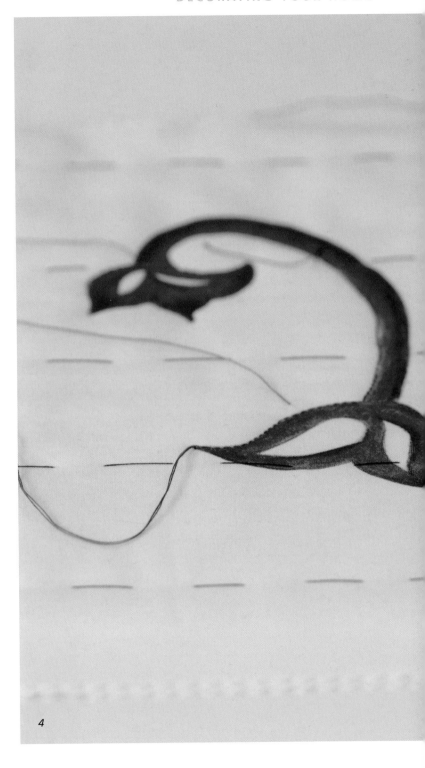

4

5

## step five

Once you have outlined every part of your design, finish off all of the threads by pulling them through to the front of the quilt. Tie each pair of threads in a knot at the fabric surface. Thread the ends into a needle and pass the thread between the layers, pulling the knot into the batting. Bring the needle back to the surface and snip off the threads at the fabric surface.

Use a white cotton thread to quilt the background of the quilt. A small all-over stipple pattern flattens out the background, making the colored areas puff out like a trapunto design.

Trim the edges of your quilt evenly around the design, adding a ¼in (6mm) allowance on all sides. Take the binding strips you set aside in step one and join them using bias joins to make one long strip. Bind the quilt according to the detailed instructions on page 125–7.

### step six

Follow the manufacturer's instructions to apply
the sapphire Swarovski crystals to the quilt top.
Be careful with your tools: the applicator wand tip
gets very hot, so make sure you have a safe place
to rest it between uses.

Turn the wand on, and allow it to heat up. When
the applicator wand is ready, slide the Swarovski
crystal in gently, hold it until the glue pad begins
to get shiny and bubble, and then tap it onto the
surface of the fabric.

Place the crystals in the small blank areas inside the
design, placing a single crystal in circular areas or
a row of crystals in crescent-shaped areas. Refer to
the picture for placement.

6

# blooming beauties

*Constructed to be useful as well as beautiful, quilted bowls are true works of art.*

These quirky bowls are a cute way of turning your quilting skills to other purposes. You could use them to hold decorative items, such as seashells, painted eggs, or a button collection. A bright, quilted bowl is the perfect receptable for house keys, mobile phones and all those other items that get tossed down on the kitchen bench and lost. Or you could simply leave them empty and admire the pretty shapes and colours they display.

### materials and techniques

Quilting fabric and batting together gives a structure that can be surprisingly sturdy. On a small scale, as with the bowls on these pages, quilted items will hold their shape quite well without any special stiffeners. The secret is on the inside: heavyweight fusible batting provides solid support to the fabric. Satiny buttonhole stitches complete the construction with smooth strength.

*Filled with joy or junk, these cheery quilted bowls will brighten your day.*

# blooming beauties

## materials

*12½in (32cm) square of hot pink cotton fabric*

*12½in (32cm) square of pale pink cotton fabric*

*2½in x 21½in (6cm x 54cm) green cotton fabric*

*3in x 5½in (7cm x 14cm) bright yellow cotton fabric*

*16in (40cm) heavyweight fusible batting*

*12½in (32cm) double-sided fusible interfacing*

*Hot pink, green and bright yellow machine sewing*
*thread to match fabrics*

*Tracing paper*

*Template plastic or thin card*

*2B pencil or tailor's chalk*

*Sharp 80 sewing machine needle*

*Basic sewing equipment (see page 110)*

*Basic quilting equipment (see page 113)*

## step one

From the double-sided fusible interfacing, cut a 12½in (32cm) square; a 3in x 5½in (7cm x 14cm) strip; and a 2½in x 10⅝in (6cm x 27cm) strip. From the heavyweight fusible batting, cut two 12½in (32cm) squares and a 2½in x 21½in (6cm x 54cm) strip.

Trace the patterns for the flower, centre circle and leaves from page 138 onto tracing paper. Retrace them onto template plastic or thin card and cut out the shapes.

Follow the manufacturer's instructions and fuse a batting square to the wrong side of each pink fabric square. Lay the double-sided fusible interfacing, paper side up, on the batting side of one of the fabric squares. Following the manufacturer's instructions, use an iron to fuse the interfacing to the batting. Remove the paper backing and place the other square with the fabric side facing up over the first square. Press with the iron to fuse the two fabric squares together with the layers of batting sandwiched between them.

Fuse the 2½in x 21½in (6cm x 54cm) strip of batting to the wrong side of the green fabric. Cut this piece in half to give two pieces each measuring 2½in x 10⅝in (6cm x 27cm). Use the 2½in x 10⅝in (6cm x 27cm) piece of double-sided fusible interfacing to join the two pieces of green fabric and batting as you did before.

2

3

### step two

Using the template, trace the circle for the flower center twice onto the paper side of the 3in x 5½in (7cm x 14cm) strip of double-sided fusible interfacing. Follow the manufacturer's instructions and fuse the interfacing onto the wrong side of the yellow fabric. Cut out the circles, remove the paper backing and set aside.

Fold the layered square into quarters. Finger press the folds to mark the center. Fold and finger press a circle in the same way. Matching center points, center the circle over the square with the right side facing up. Press to fuse it in place. Machine stitch around the outside of the circle close to the edge. Turn the fabric over and place the remaining yellow circle, fusible-side down, inside the stitching line. Press to fuse it in place.

### step three

Set the sewing machine to the widest zigzag stitch and the stitch length to the buttonhole setting. Test the stitching on a scrap of fabric: you want the stitches to be as close together as possible. Using yellow thread to match the flower centre, buttonhole stitch around the circle. To hide the ends of the threads, pull them through to one side, thread them into a needle and pass them through the batting layer for a short distance. Cut the threads close to the fabric surface. Transfer the pattern from page 138 onto the top side of the bowl, continuing the straight lines between the petals out to the edges of the fabric. Using hot pink thread to match the fabric, stitch the inner petals with straight stitch. Use a rotary cutter to cut the straight lines of the pattern and remove the "V"s of fabric between the petals.

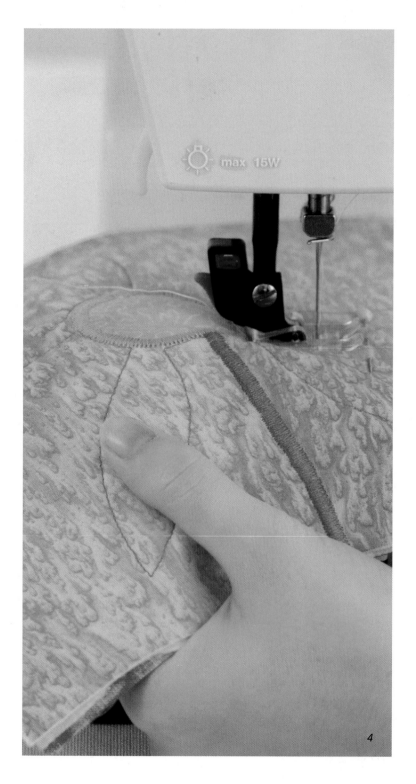

### step four

Hold the adjacent edges of the petals together with quilting pins or basting stitches. Using hot pink thread to match the fabric, start buttonhole stitching from the center and work out to the edge. Check the underside of the seam to ensure that all of the fabric edges are covered by stitching. If necessary, stitch over the seam again. Straight stitch around the outside edge of the bowl, on the traced lines. Trim the edge 1/16in (2mm) from the stitching line. Using the hot pink thread, buttonhole stitch around the outer edges of the petals, covering the raw edges of the fabric and batting. You may need to go around twice to achieve good coverage. Finish the thread ends as described in step three.

Transfer the leaf patterns onto the padded green fabric pieces (see step one). Include the leaf veins. Using green thread to match the fabric, straight stitch around the outside edge and continue up the leaf, stitching the lines of the veins. Trim the outside edges to within 1/16in (2mm) of the stitching. Buttonhole stitch around the edges of the leaves, repeating if necessary. Hand stitch the leaves in place on the outside of the bowl so that the stitches don't show.

# zigzag pizzazz

*Bright fabrics and geometric shapes give this cushion a jazzy feel.*

A large, comfortable cushion like this one is perfect for tossing onto a sofa, bed or even a blanket under a shady tree for a warm-weather picnic. The basic block, four of which make up the cushion, is easy to assemble and join together to great effect.

Make a set of cushions, each with slightly different colour and shape combinations, or combine multiple sets of blocks to make a matching quilt.

## materials and techniques

The sharp edges of the design of these foundation-pieced blocks are perfectly complemented by the bright purples, reds and greens, but many color combinations are possible. Stark black and white, combined with black-and-white print fabrics, would also be very effective, as would more muted shades to suit a softer décor. Foundation piecing ensures that the lines and points of this asymmetric design remain crisp and clean.

*Take a comfy cushion and a good book outdoors for a relaxing day.*

# zigzag pizzazz

## materials

4¾in (12cm) each of 15 different cotton fabrics
    in a variety of hot pink, apple green and
    purple prints

24in (60cm) square of cotton fabric for the
    cushion back

16in (40cm) zipper

3yd (2.5m) piping cord

20in (50cm) square of pink fabric for piping

Pearl cotton no. 8 in matching colors for quilting

22in (55cm) square of batting

22in (55cm) square of calico or plain cotton fabric
    for the back of the quilted top

Neutral sewing machine thread for piecing

Sewing machine thread to match back fabric

Tracing paper or baking paper

2B pencil

20in (50cm) cushion insert

Basic sewing equipment (see page 110)

Basic quilting equipment (see page 113)

## step one

Trace the pattern for the zigzag foundation piecing from page 139 onto tracing paper using a 2B pencil, marking all of the lines shown. You will need to trace four copies of the pattern, one for each block of the cushion top.

Cut 2⅜in (6cm) strips across the width of the fabrics you want to use for the zigzags (two colors for each block). Lay the strips for one block with right sides together and lay the paper pattern over the top so that the fabric completely covers the first triangle. The fabric on top, immediately under the paper, will be the first triangle, while the second fabric will form the second triangle. Make sure that at least ¼in (6mm) of fabric extends beyond the pencil lines on the pattern to form the seam allowances.

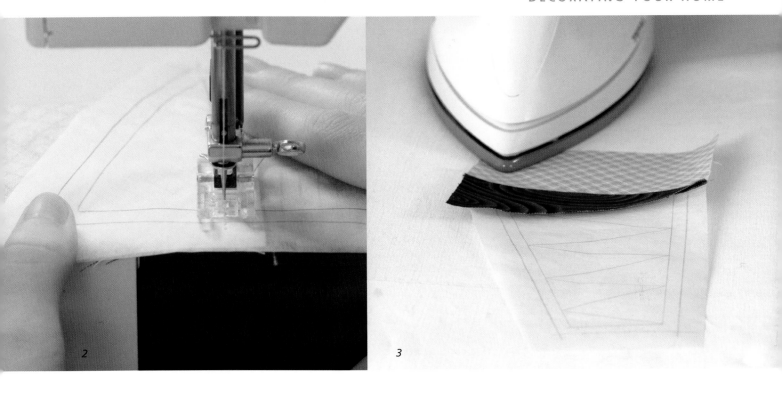

2

3

### step two

Pin the fabrics to the paper pattern and stitch along the first zigzag line as shown in the photograph. The paper pattern should be on top as you stitch. See page 116 for details on foundation piecing.

Repeat this step with the three remaining paper patterns and pairs of fabric strips.

Fold the paper pattern out of the way and trim the seam allowance to ¼in (6mm): you may do this with scissors or with a rotary cutter. Do not cut the paper pattern at this stage.

### step three

Turn the pattern with the fabric attached over to the right side and fold the second fabric strip out so that both fabrics have the right side up. Press carefully to flatten the seam. You may wish to trim away excess fabric from the front edge of the second fabric strip, making sure that you completely cover the next triangle on the pattern and leave at least ¼in (6mm) of fabric for the seam allowance.

Repeat this step with the three remaining paper patterns and pairs of fabric strips.

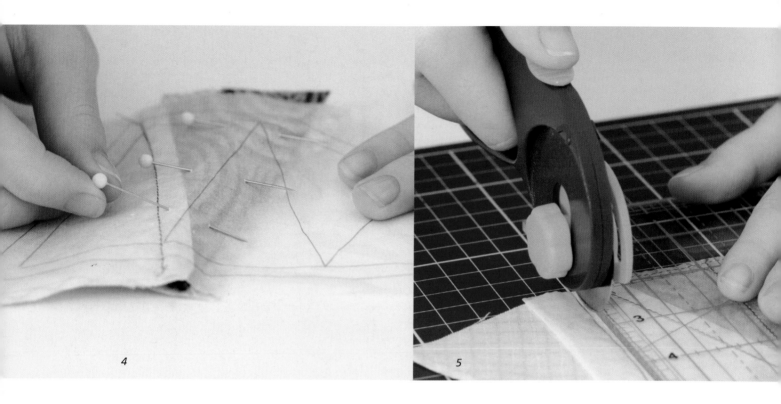

4

5

### step four

Lay the paper pattern with the attached pieces
over the strip of the first color fabric so that
the right sides are together. Ensure that there is
enough fabric in the strip to cover the next triangle
of the zigzag. Pin the strip to the paper pattern
with the pieces attached, with the edges of the
fabrics meeting at the seam allowance. Stitch
along the pencil line as before, then fold back the
paper pattern and trim the seam to ¼in (6mm).
Turn the pattern over, open out the fabric and
press the seam flat. Trim away excess fabric from
the front edge of the third fabric strip.

Repeat this step with the three remaining paper
patterns and pairs of fabric strips.

### step five

Continue alternating the two fabrics and repeating
step three until you have covered all of the triangles
on the paper pattern.

Press the completed piece so that the fabrics are all
lying flat and stitch around the outside edge of the
paper pattern, halfway between the two pencil lines.
This stitching acts as stay stitching while you work
with the block, preventing the edges of the zigzag
piece from stretching, as some of them will be on the
bias of the fabric.

Trim the zigzag piece by cutting on the outside pencil
line with a rotary cutter, giving a ¼in (6mm) seam
allowance all around.

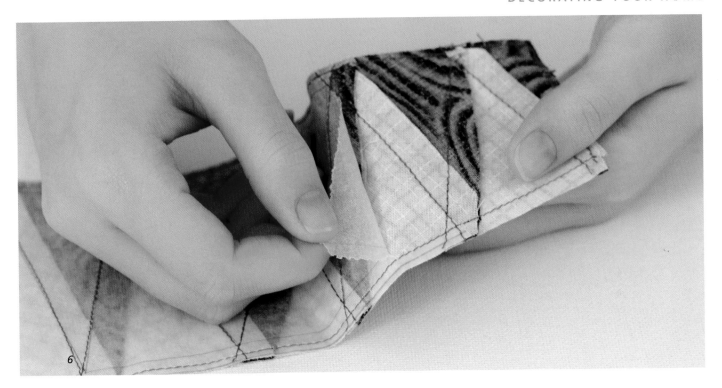

6

### step six

Remove the paper pattern carefully from the back of the zigzag piece by simply tearing along the stitching. From the remaining fabrics, cut strips 10½in (27cm) long and 2⅜–2¾in (6–7cm) wide at one end and 1¼–1½in (3–4cm) wide at the other end. Referring to the photograph on page 48, lay one of the strips along one long edge of the zigzag piece with right sides together and edges meeting. Pin and stitch a ¼in (6mm) seam along the edge, then press the seam towards the strip.

Continue to add strips of fabric around the block, working in a quirky log cabin style (see page 119 for a traditional log cabin layout). Keep adding strips until the block is larger than 10½in (27cm) in both directions. Trim the block to a 10½in (27cm) square. Repeat this step for the remaining three blocks.

Lay the four completed blocks on a flat surface and arrange them in a pleasing formation, rotating each block so the zigzags point in a different direction. Join the top two blocks and the bottom two blocks using a ¼in (6mm) seam. Press the top seam to the left and the bottom seam to the right. Now join the top blocks to the bottom blocks.

Make a quilt sandwich for the cushion front by laying the backing fabric right side down on a flat surface. Lay the batting over the top and the cushion front right side up on the top. Pin and baste the three layers together. See page 122 for instructions on making a quilt sandwich. Using pearl cotton no. 8, hand quilt just inside the seams of the quilt blocks. See page 123 for instructions on hand quilting. When you have finished quilting, trim the raw edges of all layers level with each other.

### step seven

Cut the fabric for the piping into bias strips
approximately 1¼in (3cm) wide. See page 115 for
instructions on cutting on the bias. Place the ends
of two strips with right sides together and edges
matching (the strips should form a right angle where
they overlap). Stitch across the ends of the strips using
a ¼in (6mm) seam, parallel with the edges of the
fabric, then press the seam open and trim away the
corners of the seam allowances level with the edges
of the strip. Join enough strips in this manner to go
right around the outside edge of the cushion top
(approximately 88in or 220cm).

Fold the bias strip over the piping cord with the right
side out and the edges meeting. Use a zipper foot to
stitch close to the piping cord, enclosing it in fabric.
Trim the raw edges to approximately ½in (12mm) seam
allowance. Pin the piping onto the cushion front with
the raw edges of the bias strips meeting the raw edges
of the cushion front. When you reach a corner, clip the
bias strip in the seam allowance to allow it to make a
90 degree turn. When you reach the beginning of the
piping cord, ensure that there is a small overlap of cord
and fabric.

Stitch the piping to the cushion front using a zipper
foot, leaving a small gap in the stitching where the
ends overlap.

With the piping stitched in place, trim one end of the
piping and cord straight. Leave a small amount of fabric
(about ¾in or 2cm) at the other end to overlap, but
trim the piping cord so that it buts up against the other
end of the cord. Fold over a ¼in (6mm) seam allowance
on the end of the fabric and overlap the seam over the
beginning of the fabric and cord.

### step eight

Complete the stitching using a zipper foot as before. Carefully measure the cushion front in both directions. It should measure about 19½–20½in (50–52cm) square. Cut the cushion back fabric to the same height, adding 2in (5cm) to the width. Now fold the cushion back fabric in half vertically (so that the shorter sides are together) and cut it along the fold line. Overlock or zigzag the cut edges before you begin to place the zipper.

Press a 1in (2.5cm) seam allowance under along the overlocked edges. Lay one fold along the zipper, close to the teeth. Use a zipper foot to stitch close to the edge of the fold using sewing thread to match the cushion back fabric. Lay the other fold along the opposite side of the zipper, overlapping the folded edges of the two fabric pieces slightly. Stitch along the top fold, catching the other fabric edge in the stitching, until you reach the zipper. With the machine needle in the fabric, pivot the pieces 90 degrees and stitch ⅜in (1cm) across the top of the zipper. Stitch backwards and forwards to reinforce.

With the machine needle in the fabric, pivot the pieces back to the original direction and stitch parallel to the fold along the length of the zipper. At the other end of the zipper, pivot the piece 90 degrees and stitch across to the edge of the fold, reinforcing as before. Pivot the piece back to the original direction and complete the stitching of the seam.

Open the zipper, then lay the cushion front and back with right sides together. Pin around the outside of the cushion, then stitch just inside the piping stitching line, using the sewing machine zipper foot. Overlock or zigzag stitch the raw edges together.

Clip the corners and turn the cushion cover through the open zipper to the right side. Insert a cushion, then close the zipper.

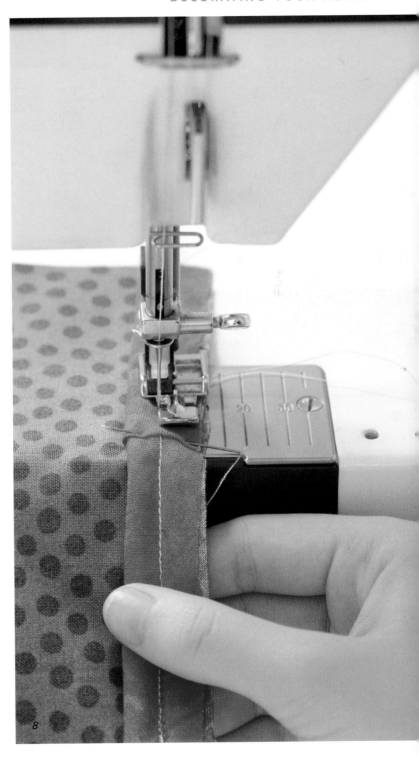

8

quilts for kids

# snuggle time

*Quick and easy to assemble, this cuddly quilt
will keep your toddler warm at night.*

Babies under one year of age don't need padded,
fluffy quilts, but once they reach toddlerhood they will
appreciate the extra comfort of a soft bed cover. You can
assemble this simple quilt in just a few hours using an
ordinary sewing machine.

### materials and techniques

Use soft cotton flannel and cotton batting for this quilt
and it will be machine washable and tumble-dryable:
wash separately on your normal cotton cycle and tumble
dry on a cool or warm setting.
The exposed raggy seams look better and better after
each wash, while tumble-drying helps to keep the quilt
nice and fluffy.

*Make this quilt in
plain or printed
flannel fabrics to
match the décor of
your child's room.*

# snuggle time

## materials

*60in (1.5m) cotton flannel (color 1 – lavender)*

*60in (1.5m) cotton flannel (color 2 – lime)*

*60in (1.5m) cotton batting*

*Polyester sewing thread to match fabrics*

*Basic sewing equipment (see page 110)*

*Basic quilting euipment (see page 113)*

*Finished size: 36in x 40in*

*(80cm x 100cm)*

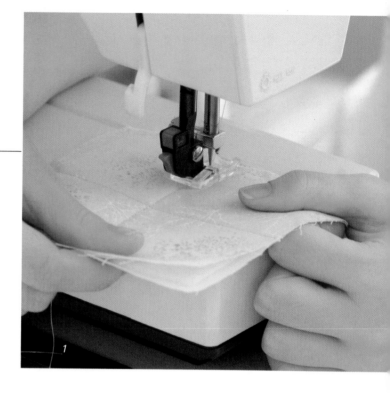

### step one

From the lavender flannel, cut 80 patches, each 5in (12.5cm) square. From the lime flannel, cut 80 patches, each 5in (12.5cm) square. From the batting, cut 80 patches, each 4in (10cm) square. Sandwich a square of batting between a square of lavender flannel and a square of lime flannel, making sure the right sides of both fabrics are facing out. Pin the layers together and, measuring with a quilting ruler, mark the centre of each edge with a pin or tailor's chalk.

Prepare a sewing machine with lime thread on top and lavender thread in the bobbin. With the lime fabric up, sew straight stitch across the centre of each sandwich in both directions.

2

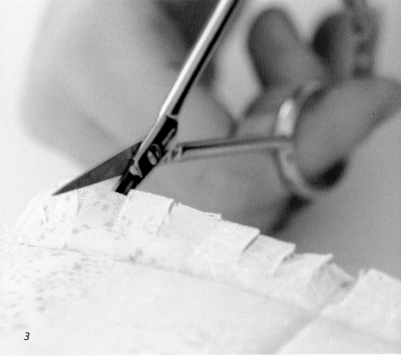

3

### step two

Begin sewing the blocks together in rows of ten.
Place two blocks together with the same colour
on top (so that the colours will alternate). Pin and
stitch along one edge using a ½in (12mm) seam
allowance. Stitch just along the edge of the batting.
Open the blocks out and place them with the seam
facing down on a flat surface. Lay the next block
on top of the right-hand block with raw edges
matching, ensuring that the colours will alternate.
Pin and stitch along the edge as before.
Continue to add blocks until you have joined ten
in a row. Make eight rows of ten blocks. Join the
rows together using the same method as for joining
the blocks, making sure you alternate the colours
in each row.

### step three

When you have joined all of the rows, stitch all the
way around the outside edge of the quilt using a
½in (12mm) seam as before.
Snip all of the raw edges of the seams back to the
stitching line at ⅜in (10mm) intervals. This helps to
promote the fluffy, ragged look. The seams are on the
top side of the quilt.
Wash and tumble-dry the quilt on a gentle cotton
cycle to fluff up the seams.

# playtime quilt

*Precut felt pieces are made up into a simple, washable play mat for a baby or a pet.*

Babies love to spend time on the floor, having their "tummy time" to help them develop strong neck muscles. On the floor they learn to roll from their back to the front as they reach for their favourite toys. A padded play mat like this one is the perfect place to put them during the early months of their development. It's so quick and easy to make, you're guaranteed to have time to finish it before they're crawling away!

### materials and techniques

Nothing could be simpler than assembling this play mat from precut felt pieces purchased from your local craft shop. Nine pieces in three different colours make a simple pattern. There is no binding, and the quilting is done by simply tying at the intersections of the seams and in the centers of the felt squares. Iron-on appliqué is optional; you can leave it off for an even faster finish.

*"Tummy time" was never so comfortable.*

# playtime quilt

## materials

*10in x 11½in (25cm x 29cm) precut craft felt pieces,*
*    three each in white, apricot and caramel*
*32in x 36in (82cm x 92cm) cream felt fabric*
*    for backing*
*32in x 36in (82cm x 92cm) thick polyester batting*
*Large safety pins*
*Machine sewing thread in a neutral colour*
*Pearl cotton no. 5 in ecru*
*Straw needle, no. 8*
*Scraps of craft felt for appliqué (optional)*
*Double-sided fusible interfacing (optional)*
*Basic sewing equipment (see page 110)*
*Basic quilting equipment (see page 113)*

*Finished size:*
**26½ in x 33½ in (67.5cm x 85cm)**

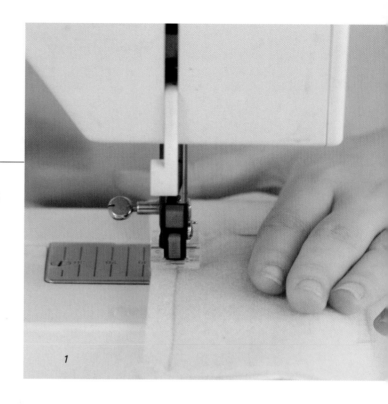

1

### step one

Lay out the felt pieces for the quilt top in three rows
of three: Row 1 – white, caramel, apricot; Row 2 –
apricot, white, caramel; Row 3 – caramel, apricot,
white. The felt pieces do not have a right and wrong
side, and the raw edges do not need to be finished to
prevent fraying. This makes the quilt assembly faster.
Take the white and caramel pieces for the top row
and stitch them together down one long edge, using
a ¼in (6mm) seam allowance. Lay the apricot piece
for the top row over the caramel piece with edges
together and stitch a ¼in (6mm) seam down the long
edge. Repeat for the remaining rows. Stitch the rows
together using a ¼in (6mm) seam allowance.

### step two

Lay the polyester batting on a flat surface, then lay the felt backing fabric on top of the batting. There is no right or wrong side of the felt, but the side facing up will become the right side.

Lay the quilt top, right-side down, on top of the backing fabric and smooth it out evenly. Pin all layers together with large safety pins, particularly at the intersections of the seams on the quilt top. Pin around the edge of the quilt top with quilting pins placed at right angles to the edges.

Machine stitch all layers together ¼in (6mm) inside the edges of the quilt top. Leave the length of one felt piece at the side edge open for turning. When the stitching is complete, trim the batting and backing fabric to the edge of the quilt top. Cut the batting back further, close to the stitching line. Clip the corners of the seam allowance off diagonally. Turn the quilt right-side out through the opening in the side. Turn the edges of the opening under and sew it closed using ladder stitch.

Tie the back and front of the quilt together. Cut thirteen 6in (15cm) lengths of ecru pearl cotton thread. Lay the quilt right-side up on a flat surface. Thread a straw needle with one length of pearl cotton and pass the needle straight down through an intersection of seams on the quilt top. Holding the end of the pearl cotton so that it does not pull through, carefully turn over the quilt and pass the needle straight back up through the quilt, 1/16in (2mm) from the original entry point. Unthread the needle and tie a secure knot on the fabric. Trim the ends of the thread 1in (2.5cm) from the knot. Repeat at the remaining seam intersections and in the center of each felt piece.

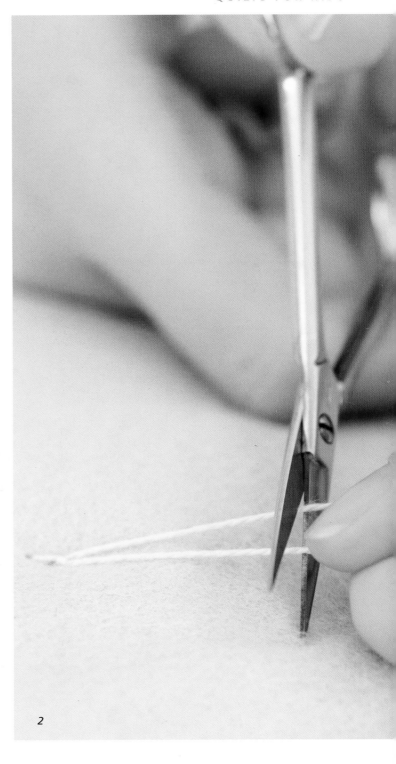

2

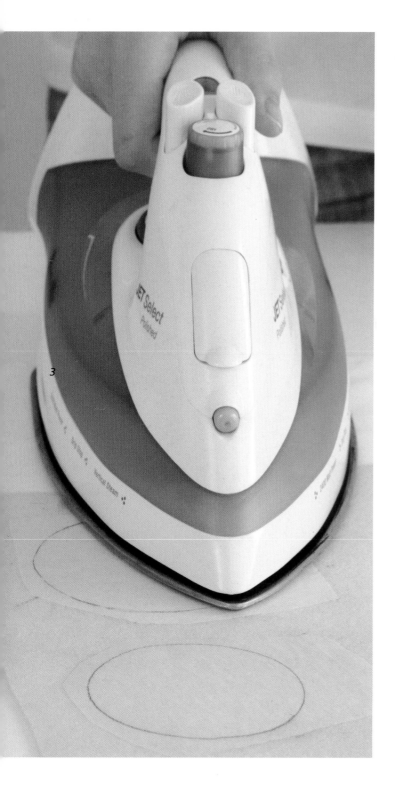

3

## step three

If you wish, you can add appliqué shapes to the basic play mat design. Circles of different sizes are simple to trace and cut.

Trace circles of various sizes onto the paper side of the double-sided fusible interfacing: use small plates and saucers, coffee cups, coins and other objects as templates. Roughly cut out the traced circles.

Lay the circles on colored felt pieces, with the paper side of the fusible interfacing up. There is no right or wrong side of the felt but there is definitely a right side of the double-sided fusible interfacing! Following the manufacturer's instructions, use an iron to fuse the interfacing to the felt.

Cut out the circles on the traced lines, cutting through the paper and felt. Remove the backing paper.

Lay the circles with the interfacing side down on the front of the play mat in a pleasing arrangement. Use a warm, dry iron to gently fuse the circles to the mat. You could use other shapes, such as triangles, squares and oblongs as well as circles.

## bumper pads

Bumper pads are another simple item you can make using precut craft felt pieces for a quick but effective result. Sew nine pieces of precut felt together in a strip, joining them at the shorter edges. Use a ¼in (6mm) seam. Make a second strip of nine pieces the same as the first one.

Use ecru grosgrain ribbon, ¼in (6mm) wide, as ties to secure the bumper to the cot. Cut sixteen 8in (20cm) lengths of ribbon. With the right side of the strips facing up (that is, with the seams facing down) pin a length of ribbon at the upper and lower corners of the ends of the strip. Pin lengths of ribbon at the upper and lower edges of the third seam from each end. Baste the ends of the ribbon to the felt. Do this on both strips of felt.

Place the two strips of felt with right sides together (and the ribbons sandwiched between them). Be careful not to let the loose ends of the ribbons get caught up in the seam allowances. Lay a strip of batting on top of the felt strips and pin all of the layers together.

Stitch the layers together along the long edge of the strip, across one end and along the other long edge. Leave one end open for turning. Trim the batting back to the stitching line and clip the corners diagonally as you did for the play mat. Turn to the right side through the open end and hand sew it closed using ladder stitch.

Quilt the bumper by carefully machine stitching along the seam lines, making sure that the seams on both front and back are exactly aligned. Tie the quilt as for the play mat in the center of each felt panel.

# building blocks

*Simply constructed of three-inch blocks,
this quilt is a cinch to assemble for a child's
first bed.*

It's the choice of fabric that gives this quilt life. A subtle color
scheme of creams, greens, cherries and berries makes it perfect for
a little girl's room, without it being too pink and prissy. Shift the
colors to creams, blues, greys and yellows and you've got a subtly
masculine quilt for a little boy's room.

## materials and techniques

The nine-patch block is one of the easiest to manage in quilting.
There are no fiddly points and strange fractions of inches to deal
with and, with accurately cut squares, no problems with getting
seams to meet.

You can use chain piecing to make the assembly even simpler. The
photographs over the page show how to do this: you simply have
all of your pairs of blocks ready to go and stitch the seams one after
the other without cutting the threads in between. This saves time
and prevents the wastage of thread on the short seams.

*Go back to basics with
these pretty variations
on nine-patch blocks.*

# building blocks

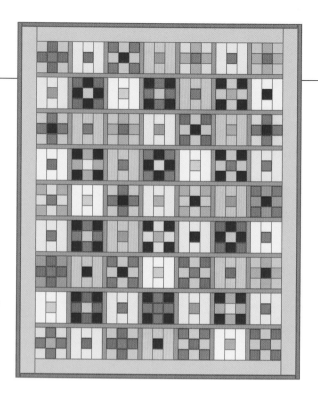

## materials

*39⅜in (1m) green floral cotton fabric*

*37⅜in (95cm) yellow floral cotton fabric*

*27½in (70cm) purple patterned cotton fabric*

*10in (25cm) orange patterned cotton fabric*

*13¾in (35cm) mottled green cotton fabric*

*16in (40cm) dark pink patterned cotton fabric*

*8in (20cm) striped yellow cotton fabric*

*10in (25cm) light pink patterned cotton fabric*

*8in (20cm) blue patterned cotton fabric*

*16in (40cm) white-and-cream striped cotton fabric*

*21⅝in (55cm) yellow-and-cream patterned*
*cotton fabric*

*16in (40cm) brown-and-cream patterned*
*cotton fabric*

*Machine sewing thread to match fabrics, such as*
*Gütermann 100% cotton thread, no 829*

*72in x 95in (180cm x 240cm) wool or polyester*
*batting*

*72in x 95in (180cm x 240cm) backing fabric*

*Safety pins*

*Basic sewing equipment (see page 110)*

*Basic quilting equipment (see page 113)*

*Finished size:*

*71in x 94½in (180cm x 240cm)*

## step one

Wash and iron all fabrics before use.

Cut strips across the width of the fabric: from green floral fabric, cut 22 strips 4cm (1½in) wide; from yellow floral fabric, cut seven strips 10cm (4in) wide; and from purple fabric, cut eight strips 5cm (2in) wide.

Cut 7.5cm (3in) squares: 43 orange squares; 46 mottled green squares; 42 purple squares; 61 dark pink squares; 22 striped yellow squares; 28 floral yellow squares; 38 light pink squares; 23 blue squares; 14 floral green squares; 18 white cream stripe squares; 25 yellow cream squares; 20 brown cream squares.

Cut 7.5cm x 20cm (3in x 8in) rectangles: 18 white-and-cream stripe; 24 yellow-and-cream; 20 brown-and-cream.

From the green floral strips, cut 54 shorter strips, each 20cm (8in) long.

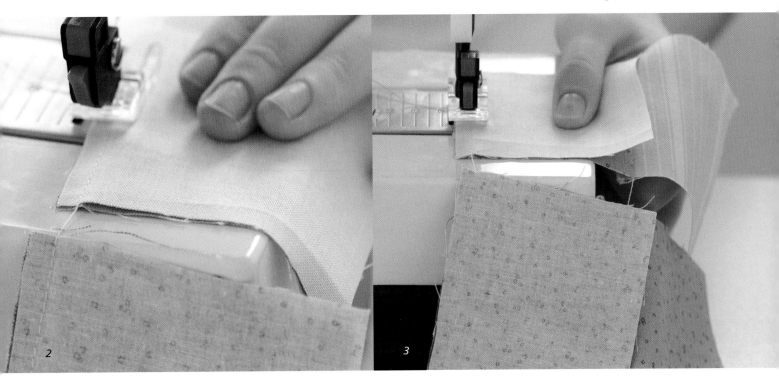

2

3

### step two

Lay out all the cut pieces on the floor or a large flat area, according to the diagram on the previous page. Use ¼in (6mm) seams throughout the quilt.

Sew each colored nine-patch block together. Use chain piecing as shown in the photograph above. Take the first two squares of each row of the block and lay them with right sides together, ready to stitch. Thread up the sewing machine and set it on a neat, short stitch length. Sew the pairs of blocks together using a ¼in (6mm) seam. As soon as you reach the end of the first pair of blocks, stop sewing, lift the presser foot and place the second pair of blocks under the presser foot, in line with the first pair. Return the presser foot to the down position and stitch the seam of the second pair of blocks. Repeat with the third pair. This will give three pairs of blocks with a short length of thread between each pair.

### step three

Open out the pairs of blocks and press the seams to alternate sides.

Take the chain pieced patches and add the third patch to each row by placing it right-side down on top of the center patch. Chain piece as before and press the seams in alternate directions. You should now have three rows of three patches, joined with short lengths of thread between the seams.

There is no need to cut the threads before moving on to the next step.

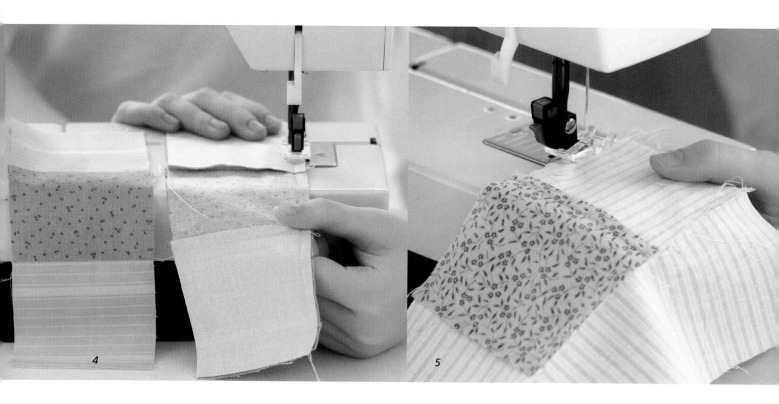

4

5

### step four

Without cutting the threrads between the rows, turn the top row of three patches over so that it sits on top of the second row with the seams aligned. The seam allowances should face in opposite directions. Stitch the two rows together using a ¼in (6mm) seam allowance. Press the seam allowance towards the second row.
Lay the two joined rows right-side down over the third row with the seams aligned. The seams should face in opposite directions. Stitch the third row to the first two to create a nine-patch block.

### step five

Sew a cream square above and below each coloured center square, according to the diagram on page 70. This will give a strip of three squares. Sew the cream rectangles lengthwise to the side edges of these strips. Lay all the assembled blocks out again according to the diagram. Sew each row of blocks together with a short strip of floral green fabric between each block.
Join the remaining floral green strips together to create one very long strip. From this strip, cut eight strips each 59in (150cm) long. Sew the rows of blocks together, with a long floral green strip in between each row.
Join all the floral yellow strips together to create one very long strip. From the strip, cut two strips 59in (150cm) long, and two strips 83in (211cm) long.
Sew the shorter yellow strips to the upper and lower edges of the quilt top. Sew the long strips to the side edges.

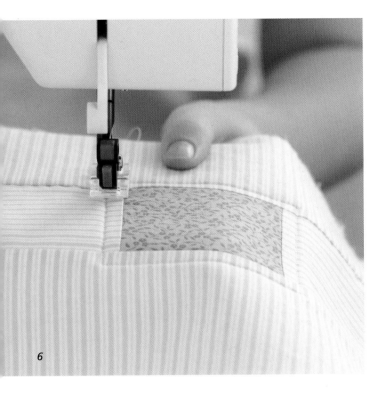

6

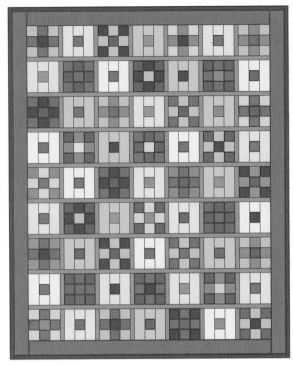

### step six

On a large flat surface (such as a clean floor or table), lay the backing fabric right-side down. Lay the batting on top, then the assembled quilt top right-side up to create a quilt sandwich (see page 122 for more details). Using safety pins, pin around the edge of the quilt, every 8–12in (20–30cm). Place a pin at the center of each block. Place a pin in the intersections the floral green strips.

Baste around the edge of the entire quilt. Baste from one edge of the quilt to the other at 2½in (6.5cm) intervals, making a grid across the whole quilt. Remove all safety pins.

Machine quilt with a straight stitch ¼in (6mm) outside the center square of each block and ¼in (6mm) inside the outer edge of each block. The photograph shows the quilting being worked on a single block.

On the yellow border, quilt ¼in (6mm) from the edges closest to the pieced blocks.

Trim the batting and backing fabric back level with the edge of the quilt top.

Join all the purple strips together using diagonal seams to create one very long strip. Fold in half along the length of the strip. With raw edges together, stitch the purple binding strip to the edge of the quilt, mitring the corners as you reach them. (See page 125–7 for more detailed instructions on binding a quilt.)

Turn the quilt over and hand stitch the folded edge of the binding to the stitching on the back of the quilt.

*Above: Try a different colour combination to make a version of this quilt for a boy. The variation above is just one suggestion.*

# bendy bay

*Friendly rays and quirky octopuses adorn a quilt for hanging on the wall or draping over a chair.*

The underwater environment is a fascinating place for a child's imagination to explore. A place where fish can breathe but mammals can't, where creatures float above the earth without wings, where beautiful and strange animals make their homes. What child – or adult – can resist such an extraordinary world? This simple wall quilt will inspire stories, imaginings and investigations for years to come.

### materials and techniques

A mottled blue fabric makes the perfect watery background. Contrasting orange–yellow fabric is used for the appliqué, forming squiggly shapes as though they are distorted by water. Needleturn appliqué is the method used here; however, a quick and easy alternative would be to use double-sided fusible interfacing and buttonhole stitch to sew it down.

*Gone fishin': a bright quilt can be a great comfort on a sunny afternoon by the pond.*

# bendy bay

**materials**

*43¼in (110cm) squares of two contrasting hand-dyed cotton fabrics, one for the base and one for the appliqué*

*43¼in (110cm) square of backing fabric*

*43¼in (110cm) square of batting*

*8in (20cm) blue fabric for the binding*

*Cotton sewing thread to match fabrics*

*Pearl cotton no. 8 to match the base fabric*

*2B pencil or tailor's chalk*

*Large piece of cardboard (at least 22in or 55cm square)*

*Blunt-nose embroidery scissors (optional)*

*Basic sewing equipment (see page 110)*

*Basic quilting equipment (see page 113)*

*Finished size:*

*43in x 43in (109cm x 109cm) square*

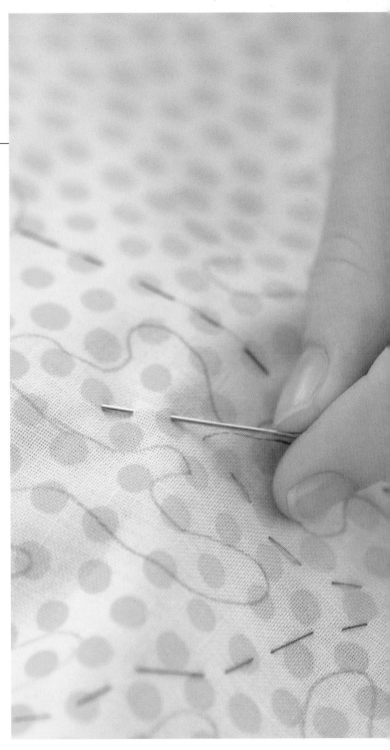

### step one

Enlarge and transfer the quarter pattern from page 140 onto cardboard.

Fold the quilt top fabrics into quarters and press the folds. Lay the two fabrics right-side up and baste them together along the pressed creases, dividing the quilt top into quarters. Baste around the outside edges as well.

Carefully cut out the coral shape in the center of the pattern from the cardboard. Lay this template onto the center of one of the quarters of the quilt, aligning the straight edges of the template with the basting lines.

Trace the shape of the template with a 2B pencil or tailor's chalk, as you prefer.

Flip the template over. Align it with the center of the next quarter of the quilt and trace the shape. Continue around all four quarters of the quilt.

Carefully cut out the octopus shape and trace an octopus onto each of the quarters. Retain the section of the cardboard pattern between the coral and the octopus and use it as a template to get the position of the octopus correct. Remember to flip the templates over so that each image is a mirror of the one in the previous quarter.

Next, cut out the stingray shapes and trace them onto each quarter. Retain the section of the cardboard pattern between the octopus and the rays to use as a template to get the position correct. Cut out the bubbles and trace them onto the fabric.

Cut out the border shape and trace it onto the edges of the quilt top. Flip the cardboard over to ensure that each quarter is a mirror image of the previous one.

2

### step two

Baste with running stitches inside all of the traced shapes. Make sure that all of the points of the coral, all of the legs of the octopuses and all of the stingrays' tails are basted down.

Starting in the center with the coral shape, carefully clip around the outside of the pencil line, leaving a ¼in (6mm) seam allowance. Be careful not to cut through the blue base fabric. A small pair of embroidery scissors with a blunt end is ideal for this job.

Cut the fabric away in sections and complete the appliqué in each quarter (see step three) before cutting any more fabric away. This prevents fraying if the quilt is left too long between cutting and stitching.

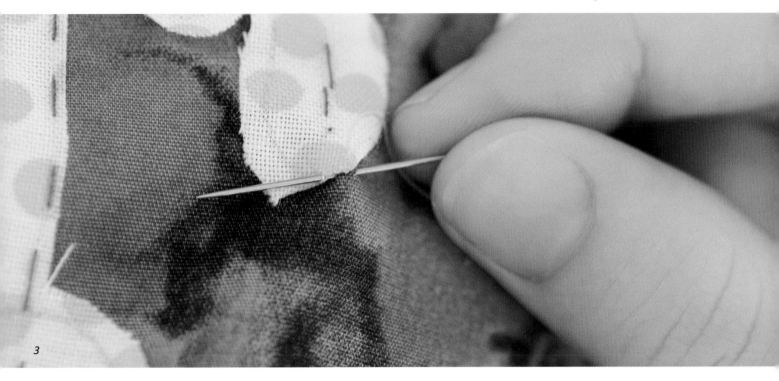

*3*

## step three

Clip the seam allowance of the curved edges at a 90
degree angle to the outline. Turn the edges of the fabric
under and stitch them down using needleturn appliqué
stitch (see page 121). When each quarter is finished,
repeat step two for the next quarter.

Cut some tiny circles of scrap fabric and appliqué them
down for the octopuses' eyes.

Press the finished quilt top carefully.

Lay the backing fabric, right-side down, on a flat surface.
Smooth the batting over the backing fabric, then lay the
quilt top right-side up on top, making a quilt sandwich
(see page 122). Baste the three layers together with
regularly spaced safety pins.

Using pearl cotton no. 8, hand quilt close to the appliqué
edges.  Echo quilt another row of stitching ¼in (6mm)
from the previous row and parallel to it. See page 123 for
more details on hand quilting. Continue echo quilting
until the base fabric is completely covered with stitching.
Trim the edges of the backing fabric and batting level
with the edges of the quilt top. Cut four 2in (5cm) wide
strips across the width of the binding fabric. Measure
the quilt through the center horizontally and cut two of
the binding strips to this measurement. Press the binding
in half lengthwise and place the binding on top of the
upper and lower edges of the quilt with raw edges
aligned. Stitch the binding to the quilt. Measure the
quilt vertically through the center and cut the remaining
binding strips to this measurement. Press the strips in
half lengthwise and stitch them to the side edges of
the quilt. Fold the binding over and slip stitch it to the
stitching on the back of the quilt. (For more details on
binding a quilt, see pages 125–7.)

# musical tote bag

*Score a hit with a quilted bag, the perfect size for sheet music and small instruments.*

Bringing your music books to piano lessons will be a pleasure when you have this great bag to carry them in. The piano keys and music staff on the front are complemented by a treble clef appliqué on the back of the bag.

### materials and techniques

The graphic ebony and ivory of the piano keys in this appliqué design is perfectly complemented by the striking red fabric making up the background. You could mimic an antique piano by using chocolate brown and cream fabric for the keys. Team that with antique gold or a rich green instead of the red background for a vintage look.

*Make merry music with this cheerful carry-all.*

# musical tote bag

## materials

*31½in (80cm) fusible quilt batting*

*10⅝in x 16½in (27cm x 43cm) white cotton self-print fabric*

*24in (60cm) red cotton fabric*

*20in (50cm) black print cotton fabric*

*6yd 20in (6m) black fusible cotton bias tape*

*6 black buttons, ¾in (2cm) diameter, with shanks*

*8in (20cm) double-sided fusible interfacing*

*24in (60cm) cotton print fabric for lining*

*Black sewing thread*

*2B pencil or temporary fabric marking pen*

*3⅜in x 12in (8.5cm x 30cm) plastic or cardboard for base*

*Basic sewing equipment (see page 110)*

*Basic quilting equipment (see page 113)*

**Finished size:**

**17¾in deep x 15in wide (45cm x 38cm)**

**step one**

From fusible quilt batting, cut two pieces for the
bag front and back each measuring 16in x 20½in
(41cm x 52cm). Cut two pieces of fusible batting
2¾in x 30¾ in (7cm x 78cm) for the straps.
Cut a piece of white print fabric 10in x 16in
(25cm x 41cm). From the red fabric, cut a piece
measuring 11¾in x 16in (30cm x 41cm) and a piece
measuring 9½in x 20½in (24cm x 52cm). From the
black fabric, cut a piece measuring 7½in x 20½in
(19cm x 52cm). Cut two pieces of the black print fabric
each measuring 5½in x 30¾in (14cm x 78cm) for
the straps.
Cut two pieces of lining fabric each measuring
16in x 20½in (41cm x 52cm).
Following the manufacturer's instructions for the
fusible batting, press the piece of white cotton fabric
to the top half of one of the pieces of fusible batting.
Be careful not to move the iron onto the exposed area
of the fusible batting.
Enlarge the pattern on page 141 and transfer the
straight lines for the piano keys onto the white fabric
using a pencil or temporary fabric marking pen.

**step two**

Cut the black fusible bias tape to cover the marked lines.
Cut seven of the lengths short (5½in or 14cm) to allow
for the black keys. Center the tape over the pencil lines.
Following the manufacturer's instructions, iron the tape
into position.
Machine stitch the tape in place, stitching close to the
edge on either side.
Trace the pattern for the black keys onto the paper side
of the double-sided fusible interfacing to give seven black
keys. Cut the shapes out of the fusible interfacing, leaving
about ³⁄₁₆in (5mm) of extra paper around the edges.
Following the manufacturer's instructions, iron the
double-sided fusible interfacing to the wrong side of the
remaining piece of the black print fabric. Use a rotary
cutter and ruler to cut along the pencil lines.

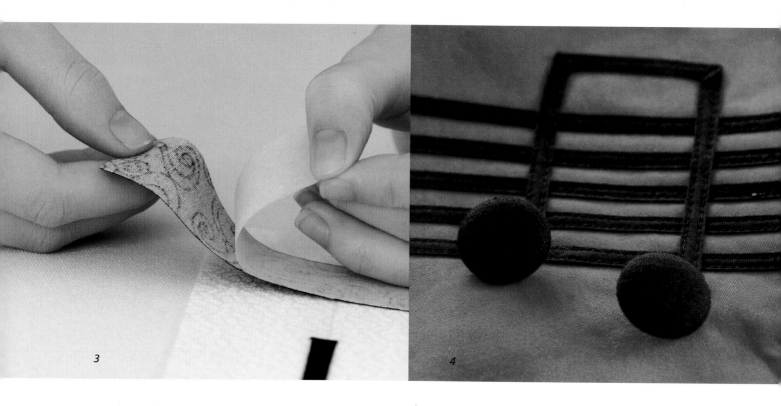

3

4

## step three

Remove the paper from the black keys and position them on the fabric keyboard using the pattern as a guide. Iron the black keys into position.

Set the sewing machine to zigzag stitch. The stitch length and width should be the same settings as for machine buttonhole stitch. Stitch around the black key shapes, leaving the lower edge free where the black and white fabric meet the fusible batting.

With right sides together, lay the 11¾in x 20½in (30cm x 52cm) piece of red fabric over the keyboard section, with raw edges aligned. Stitch a ⅜in (1cm) seam through all layers along the lower edge of the keyboard.

## step four

Open out the fabric and carefully press the red fabric, fusing it to the batting on the lower half of the bag front. Top stitch along the edge of the red fabric parallel with the seam, using the edge of the sewing machine foot as a guide.

Pin five lines of black fusible bias tape onto the red fabric for the music staff, using the pattern on page 141 as a guide. Make the lines gently curved. Press the tape into position, following the manufacturer's instructions. Stitch close to both edges of the lines of tape.

Cut six short lengths of fusible bias tape for the musical notes' stems and press them into position. Use some extra short pieces to turn some of the crotchets into quavers. Stitch along the edges of the tape as before. Attach six black buttons to complete the notes.

## step five

Press the 7½in x 20½in (19cm x 52cm) piece of black fabric to the left side of the remaining piece of fusible batting, being careful not to let the iron touch the exposed batting. Lay the 9½in x 20½in (24cm x 52cm) piece of red fabric with right sides together over the black fabric, with edges aligned where they meet the batting. Stitch a ⅜in (1cm) seam.

Open out the red fabric. Carefully press the seam and fuse the fabric to the batting.

Top stitch the seam as you did for the horizontal seam on the bag front (see step four).

Enlarge the pattern for the treble clef appliqué from page 141 and transfer it onto the paper side of the double-sided fusible interfacing. You will need to reverse the motif when you do this so that it will be the right way around when you cut it out of the fabric. Cut out the treble clef shape roughly, leaving a ⅜in (5mm) allowance around the outside edges.

Iron the treble clef shape onto the wrong side of the remaining black fabric. Cut out the shape on the pencil line. Be careful removing the internal pieces of fabric: use sharp-pointed embroidery scissors. Remove the backing paper and iron the motif into position on the red fabric, using the pattern as a guide for placement.

Use zigzag stitch set to buttonhole settings to appliqué carefully around the edges of the shape as for the black keys.

6

### step six

Following the manufacturer's instructions, fuse the strips of batting to the center of the black fabric strips on the wrong side of the fabric. Press the fabric edges towards the center of the batting so that they meet in the middle. Fold the straps in half along this line, with the raw edges on the inside of the fold.

Top stitch the straps close to the edges on both sides. Stitch again, parallel to the top stitching, using the sewing machine foot as a guide to the distance. You will now have two rows of stitching on both edges of the straps.

Check that both straps are the same length and trim the ends if necessary.

Cut the top edges of the bag front and back into the curved shape indicated on the pattern on page 141.

### step seven

Pin the ends of one strap to each side of the bag top at the outside edge of the curve, ensuring that the raw edges of the straps align with the top edge of the bag. The edges of the straps should be ⅜in (1cm) from the edge of the curves to allow for the seams. Make sure the straps are not twisted before you stitch.

Stitch the straps in place using the width of the sewing machine foot as a guide to the seam allowance, so that the stitching will be covered by the ⅜in (1cm) seam when the bag is assembled.

Pin the bag front and back together with right sides facing. Stitch down one side edge, across the lower edge and up the other side. Lay the side seam and the lower edge seam together at the corners to make a point. Stitch across the corner, 1¾in (4.5cm) from the point, to create a squared-off base for the bag. Turn the bag right side out.

Pin the two lining pieces with right sides together. Stitch both of the sides and part way across the lower edge, leaving an opening to turn the bag through after you have assembled it. Square off the base in the same way as for the bag. Cut the top edges of the lining to match the curved shape of the bag.

Slip the lining, still wrong side out, over the outside of the bag and pin the top edges together with the handles between the two layers. Stitch them together around the top edge using a ⅜in (1cm) seam allowance. Stop sewing with the needle in the fabric to turn the corners at the ends of the curves. Trim the corners and clip the curves. Turn the bag right-side out through the opening in the base of the lining. Turn the seam allowance under and machine stitch close to the edge to close the opening. Press the top edge of the bag. Top stitch close to the edge. Stitch a second row of top stitching using the sewing machine foot as a guide to distance as before.

*8*

7

### step eight

A cardboard or plastic base will give the bag added strength and shape. Cut a piece of cardboard or plastic 3⅜in x 12in (8.5cm x 30cm). Cut a piece of fabric measuring 7¼in x 24½in (18.5cm x 62cm) from the leftover lining fabric or other scrap fabric.

Fold the fabric in half to give a piece measuring 7¼in x 12¼in (18.5cm x 31cm). Fold this piece in half again to give a piece measuring 3⅝in x 12¼in (9.25cm x 31cm).

Stitch a ¼in (6mm) seam down the long raw edges. Open out the tube of fabric so that the seam is in the centre and press the seam open. Stitch across the raw edges at one end of the tube using a ¼in (6mm) seam. Clip the corners and turn the tube so that the seams are on the inside.

Slip the cardboard or plastic into the open end. This will allow you to remove the cardboard easily if you need to launder the bag.

recycled fabrics

# reuse & recycle

*During the Depression, Australian housewives turned old suits into useful blankets, and you can do the same.*

The wagga quilt, named for the country New South Wales town of Wagga Wagga (meaning "Place of Many Crows"), was a statement of resourcefulness and ingenuity during the Depression years of the 1930s. Like the pioneering women of the American west who turned flour and feed sacks into pretty patchwork, their Australian sisters used the woollen fabrics of mens' suits to create household necessities such as blankets and rugs.

### materials and techniques

The original waggas were made of suit fabrics in squares or crazy patchwork. In this updated version, pinstripes and houndstooth checks are made a feature that is complemented by seams decorated with herringbone stitch. Raid household cupboards for outdated suits or shop at your local opportunity shop for jackets, skirts and pants in pinstripe variations. Skirts are a good choice as they tend to have larger pieces of fabric from which to cut your blocks.

The fabrics don't have to be all the same weight and fiber content, although laundering will be easier if they are all wool or wool blend.

*Give your home a great new look with recycled fabric.*

# reuse & recycle

## materials

*From six different recycled fabrics:*

**Block 1:** *28 rectangles measuring 6in x 10⅝in (15cm x 27cm)*

**Block 2:** *Seven 6in (15cm) squares*

**Block 3:** *Seven 4¾in x 6in (12cm x 15cm) rectangles*

**Block 4:** *28 squares, each 3⅜in (8.5cm) square, joined into blocks measuring 6in (15cm) square*

*6yd (5.5m) of 2in (5cm) wide fabric for border*

*80in x 36in wide (2m x 90cm wide) thin wool batting*

*63in (1.6m) backing fabric*

*5 skeins of fine embroidery wool in a colour to coordinate or contrast with the fabrics*

*Basic sewing equipment (see page 110)*

*Basic quilting equipment (see page 113)*

**Finished size:**

**39in x 56⅝in wide (99cm x 144cm)**

### step one

Assemble the blocks according to the diagram at left, using a ⅜in (1cm) seam allowance. Make the first strip by joining blocks in the following order, alternating the different fabrics: Block 3, block 1, block 4, block 1, block 1, block 1, block 2.

Make the second strip by joining blocks in the following order, alternating the different fabrics: Block 1, block 4, block 1, block 1, block 1, block 2, block 3.

Make another three strips in the same order as the first strip, and another two strips in the same order as the second strip. When all of the strips are complete, join the second strip to the first strip along one long edge. Now join another first strip to the free edge of the second strip, and continue joining the strips alternately until you have a rectangular quilt top.

### step two

Sew 2in (5cm) wide strips of the border fabric together to make two pieces approximately 60in (150cm) long and two pieces approximately 45in (115cm) long. Attach the two longer strips to the side edges of the quilt top and the shorter strips to the top and bottom edges of the quilt top, using a ⅜in (1cm) seam. Stop stitching ⅜in (1cm) from the corners of the quilt top.

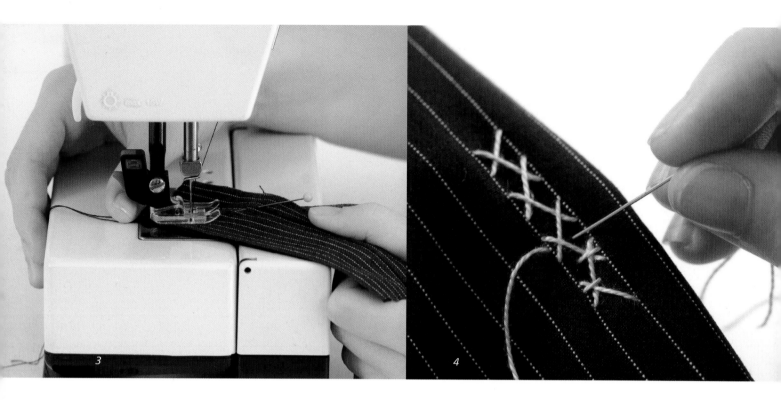

### step three

To mitre the corners of the border, fold the corner of
the quilt with right sides together, so that the side
and top edge (or side and bottom edge) are together
and the fold forms a triangle. This should bring the
unstitched ends of the border strips together as shown
in the picture. Pin or baste a seam line at an angle
across the ends of the border strips, continuing the
diagonal line of the fold. Stitch and clip the corners,
then unfold the quilt and press the corner seam open.

### step four

Using the fine embroidery wool, work over all the
seams on the quilt top in barred herringbone stitch.
This is herringbone stitch (see page 129), with a small
vertical straight stitch worked across the intersection of
the crossed threads.

5

6

## step five

Here's a tip for keeping your herringbone stitch even: take two lengths of masking tape and mark ³⁄₁₆in (5mm) intervals along one edge of each strip. Lay the masking tape on either side of the seam, about ³⁄₁₆in (5mm) from the seam. Now use the markings and the tape as a guide for your stitches.

## step six

Press the quilt top carefully, paying particular care to get the mitred corners flat and square.

With the backing fabric right side up, lay the quilt top right side down on top of the backing material, then lay the wool batting over the top. Pin and baste all three layers together and trim the batting and backing fabric level with the edges of the quilt top.

Machine stitch around all four sides of the quilt, using a ³⁄₈in (1cm) seam. Leave a small opening about 8in (20cm) wide on one side of the quilt.

Clip the corners of the seams, then turn the quilt right-side out through the opening. Carefully press the edges of the quilt to ensure a neat, square finish, and use ladder stitch to close the opening. Finally, quilt in the ditch around the seam that joins the border to the quilt top, quilting by hand or machine as you prefer.

# drop the hankie

*Vintage handkerchiefs are put to a new use in a soft and pretty quilt.*

Before the days of disposable tissues, one was not fully dressed without a handkerchief. Practical people wiped their sweaty foreheads on simple squares of cotton fabric, while those with a more refined manner wept elegantly into squares of linen edged with lace or embroidered with a stylish monogram.

A trip to the local opportunity shop will often yield a treasure trove of vintage linen. From simple squares with a machine-embroidered floral design in one corner, to lovingly handstitched and lace edged handkerchiefs, you can make a pretty collection.

### materials and techniques

When you are selecting handkerchiefs for a quilt, look for ones with lacy or scalloped edges that can be made into a feature of the quilt. With the seams on the upper side of the quilt top, these pretty features soften the edges of the squares.

*Capture the charm of yesteryear with a recycled handkerchief quilt.*

# drop the hanky

**materials**

*20 vintage handkerchiefs, washed and pressed*

*40in x 50in (102cm x 128cm) thick polycotton
   quilt batting*

*40in x 50in (102cm x 128cm) pale pink cotton
   backing fabric*

*3yd 10in (3m) pale pink 3mm wide satin ribbon*

*White sewing cotton*

*Water-soluble fabric marker or tailor's chalk*

*Basic sewing equipment (see page 110)*

*Basic quilting equipment (see page 113)*

**Finished size:**

**38½in x 48in (98cm x 122cm)**

**– size will depend on the dimensions**

**of the handkerchiefs selected.**

1

### step one

Select the smallest handkerchief and measure its dimensions. Subtract ½in (12mm) for the seam allowances: this gives you the size of the squares for the quilt. Halve this number. Fold each handkerchief in quarters and measure along the folds for the halved distance, using a water-soluble fabric marker or tailor's chalk to place a mark on the right side of the handkerchief. The mark indicates the seam allowance for each handkerchief.

Lay all of the handkerchiefs on a flat surface in four rows of five. Arrange them so that they are in a pleasing pattern. Try to alternate straight hems with scalloped or lacy borders.

Take the first two handkerchiefs and lay them with wrong sides together, aligning the marks for the seam allowances. Pin them together along one edge and machine stitch along the seam allowances. Note that the seam allowances will be slightly different for some handkerchiefs.

### step two

Press the seam open on the right side of the handkerchiefs. Take the next handkerchief in the row and lay it with wrong sides together with the previous handkerchief, aligning the seam allowances.

If a handkerchief has a plain, straight hem, lay it flat beside its neighbour with the straight edge under the decorative edge of the previous handkerchief, aligning the seam allowances. Appliqué the decorative edge over the top of the plain hem by stitching a straight line along the seam allowance.

Stitch the handkerchiefs together in rows, then stitch the rows together by aligning the seam allowances as before. Press the seams open on the right side.

2

3

## step three

When all of the handkerchiefs are joined and the seams pressed open, measure across the quilt top horizontally and vertically. Cut the batting to this size. Lay the backing fabric right-side down on a flat surface. Lay the batting over the top of the backing fabric and pin the two layers together temporarily. Trim the backing fabric to within 2in (5cm) of the edge of the batting. Fold the edges of the backing fabric over the edge of the batting and pin in place. Baste around the edges of the backing fabric and batting, about 1in (2.5cm) from the outer edge. Remove all of the pins that were holding the layers together, or they will be stitched into the quilt.

Lay the quilt top right-side down on a flat surface and lay the batting and backing fabric right-side up on top, aligning the edges of the backing with the seam allowances of the quilt top. Pin all layers together. Stitch around the edges of the backing, through all layers. Stitch ¹⁄₁₆in (2mm) from the edge of the backing. Turn the quilt over.

Cut the pink ribbon into 12 lengths and tie a tiny bow (about 1in or 2.5cm wide) in each. Using white sewing cotton and a quilting betweens needle, stitch a bow to each of the corner intersections on the quilt top. Stitch right through all of the layers of the quilt and finish off the ends of the threads under the decorative seams on the quilt top.

# scrap happy

*Raid your stash for a selection of bright fabrics to make this cute and cuddly quilt.*

A quilter's stash is often a source of delight for the whole family. Browsing through stacks of fabrics, they will recognise the remains of well-loved quilts and projects that have graced the homes of family and friends over the years. This project is ideal for using up leftovers and favourite fabrics.

### materials and techniques

Technically, this quilt does not use recycled fabrics. The materials are new, but chosen from an existing stash rather than bought especially for the project. If you want to use truly recycled fabrics, ensure that they are washed and pressed well before you begin.

*Bright colours jumble cheerfully together in the slightly wonky blocks of this quilt.*

# scrap happy

**materials**

6yd (5.5m) assorted strips of cotton fabric 2–3in (5–7.5cm) wide

18in (50cm) purple spotted cotton fabric for border one

10½in (27cm) orange print cotton fabric for border two

10½in (27cm) yellow spotted cotton fabric for border three

1yd 31in (1.7m) each of two different cotton fabrics for the backing

70in x 90in (170cm x 230cm) medium weight batting

Pearl cotton no. 8 in red, green and yellow

Neutral coloured sewing thread

2B pencil or tailor's chalk

15½in square ruler (optional)

Basic sewing equipment (see page 110)

Basic quilting equipment (see page 113)

*Finished size:*
*62in x 82½in (157cm x 210cm);*
*block size 15in x 15in (35cm x 35cm)*

1

### step one

Cut the assorted fabrics into strips across the fabric. The strips can be various sizes from 1¼in (3cm) to 2½in (6.5cm) wide.

Stitch six strips of varying widths together along the long edges, to give a minimum length of 8in (20cm) across the width of the fabric. Trim the pieced strips into maximum 8½in (21.5cm) lengths. Make fifteen strips each 8–8½in wide.

Cut the strips into right-angled triangles in the following manner. Align the 45 degree line on your quilting ruler with the straight cut edge of the strips and cut with the rotary cutter. Each strip should yield four full-sized triangles.

Lay out the triangles to make squares, each consisting of four triangles. Try to ensure that you don't use triangles from the same strip in each square. Lay out a total of 15 squares.

Press the seams of opposite triangles in the same direction. Press the seams of adjacent triangles in the opposite direction.

### step two

Pin and stitch the triangles together, ensuring that the adjacent seams lie in opposite directions. The seams will not always meet at the seam edges: this is part of the charm of the design.

Press the finished block and trim it to 15½in (39.5cm) square if necessary.

Lay all the blocks out on a flat surface in five rows of three. Stitch the blocks of each row together using a ¼in (6mm) seam. Press the seams of each row in alternate directions. Stitch the rows together.

From the purple spotted fabric for border one, cut seven 2in (5cm) strips across the with of the fabric. From the orange print fabric for border two, cut seven 1½in (4cm) strips across the width of the fabric. From the yellow spotted fabric for border three, cut seven 1½in (4cm) strips across the width of the fabric. Stitch

the pre-cut border strips together at the short ends and press the seams open.

Measure the quilt top horizontally through the center. Cut two lengths of the purple strip to this measurement and stitch to the upper and lower edges of the quilt top. Press the seams towards the outside edge of the quilt.

Measure the quilt vertically through the center including the purple borders. Cut two lengths of the remaining purple border strip to this measurement. Stitch these two strips to the side edges of the quilt. Press the seams towards the outside edge of the quilt.

Repeat with the orange print fabric for border two, then with the yellow spotted fabric for border three.

For an even more scrappy look, reduce the widths of the borders and add one or two more borders in other fabrics from your stash.

### step three

Stitch the two backing fabrics together to give a single backing piece measuring 1yd 31in x 2yd 14⅝in (170cm x 220cm). This backing piece will also be the quilt binding.

Lay the backing fabric right side down on a flat surface. Smooth the batting over the top and lay the pressed quilt top, right-side up, on top to make a quilt sandwich (see page 122). Baste the layers together with sewing thread in a 3–4in (7.5–10cm) grid.

Use tailor's chalk or a pencil to draw a series of overlapping circles on the quilt top. A dinner plate makes a good template. Hand quilt around these circles using the pearl cotton threads. (See page 123 for further instructions on hand quilting.)

When the quilting is complete, trim the batting to the edge of the quilt top. Trim the backing fabric

1in (2.5cm) larger all the way around. Turn the backing fabric over by ½in (12mm), then turn it over again to give a ½in (12mm) binding on top of the quilt. Using the pearl cotton no 8, stitch along the folded edge of the binding through all the layers. Use a small running stitch as for the quilting.

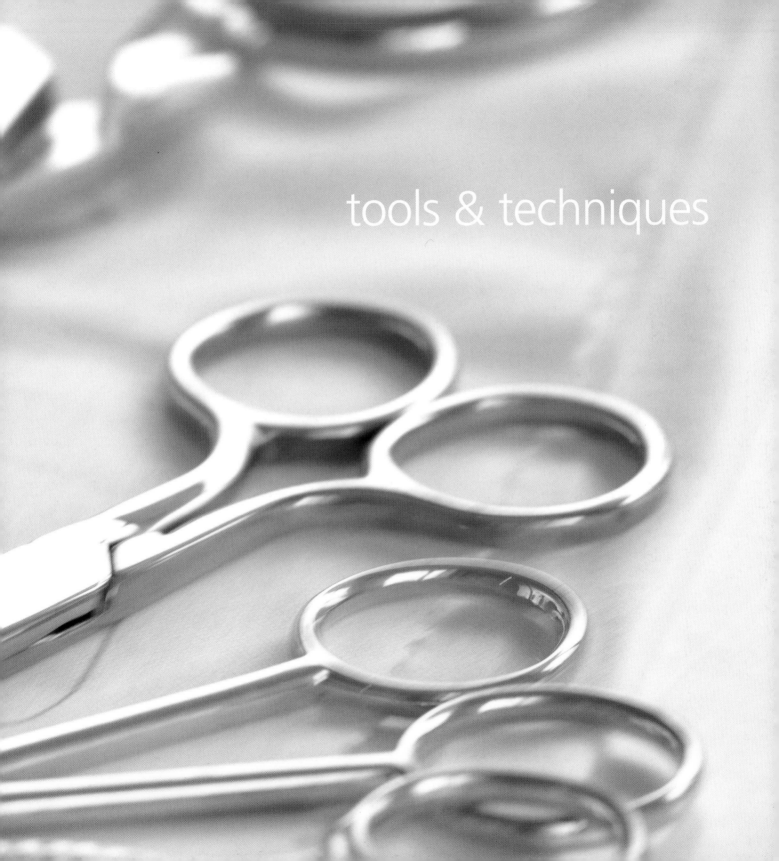

tools & techniques

# basic sewing equipment

*This list of essential accessories will ensure you've got the right tools at hand for the projects in this book and many other stitching tasks.*

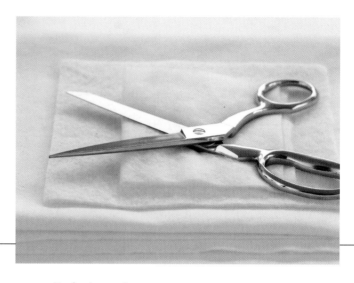

**Fabric scissors.**
Do not use fabric scissors to cut paper or other materials, as this will blunt the blades more quickly.

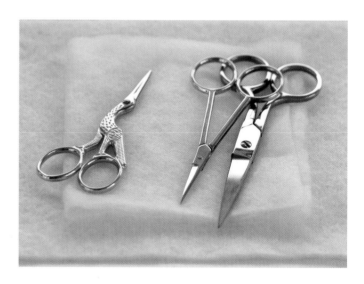

**Scissors.**
A pair of embroidery scissors with sharp points for snipping fine threads and small stitches is essential: stork scissors are a popular and decorative choice, but plain scissors do the job just as well. A pair of medium-sized, multipurpose scissors are handy for cutting paper patterns and other jobs.

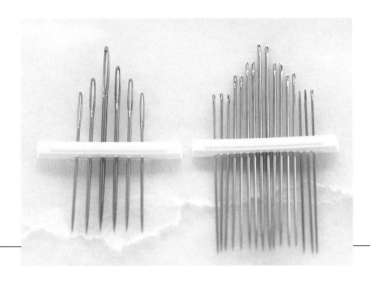

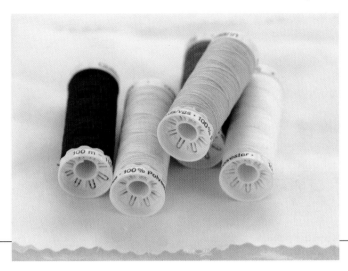

### Sewing needles.

A selection of different sizes is a good start. Most of the projects in this book will specify a size and style of needle, so you will soon add to your basic collection. There are several types of needle:

- Crewel needles are sharp pointed needles with small eyes, suitable for embroidery and other hand sewing.
- Tapestry needles have a large eye and a rounded point, for working on evenweave fabric.
- Chenille needles have a large eye and a sharp point, and are suitable for silk ribbon embroidery and working with textured threads.
- Straw needles have a small, round eye and the eye end is the same diameter as the shaft.
- Betweens needles are short, fine needles suitable for hand quilting.
- Beading needles are extra fine needles that will easily pass through the center of beads.

### Sewing thread.

Start your collection with cotton and polyester thread in black, white and ecru. Other colours can be purchased to match fabrics for your projects.

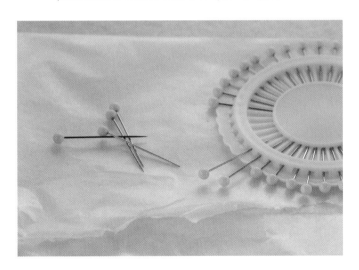

### Pins.

Choose good quality, steel-plated pins with fine shafts. Start with basic fine steel pins and add quilting pins, silk pins and any others you require for your various projects as necessary.

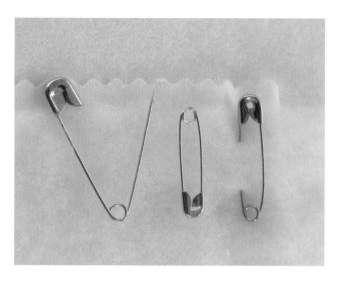

### Safety pins.

A selection of sizes will come in handy for many tasks, including fastening project pieces together so they don't get separated from each other and lost.

### Thimble.

This may seem somewhat old-fashioned but after you've pricked your finger a few times you'll wish you had one!

### Sewing machine.

A basic machine that is capable of straight stitching as well as zigzag and buttonhole stitching is all you will need for the projects in this book. If you've never used a sewing machine before, read the manufacturer's instruction booklet carefully.

### Iron and ironing board.

Most households are equipped with this essential. A steam iron with settings for the various fabrics you will be using is a good investment. A pressing cloth is another good investment: you can find these at your local craft supply store.

### Water-soluble fabric marker or tailor's chalk.

Both of these are easily removed from fabric. A sharp HB or 2B pencil can be used instead.

# basic quilting equipment

*In addition to the basic sewing equipment, the following specialised accoutrements are useful for quilters and those who dabble in the craft.*

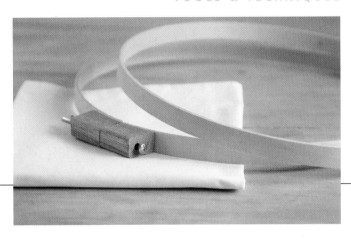

**Quilting hoop.**
Larger than an embroidery hoop, a quilting hoop is useful for keeping the quilt sandwich taut while you hand stitch the quilting.

**Self-healing cutting mat.**
Marked with a one-inch grid, this rubber mat is a safe surface for cutting fabric with a rotary cutter.

**Rotary cutter.**
The very sharp circular blades on this useful tool allow accurate cutting of fabric.

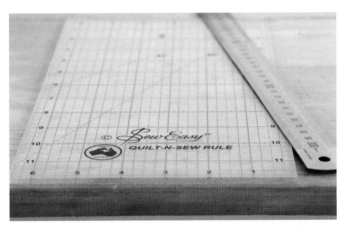

**Quilting ruler.**
A clear Perspex ruler with markings in inches as well as angled cutting lines to help when you need to cut bias strips and triangles. A metal ruler marked in inches and centimetres is also useful and can withstand the blade of a rotary cutter.

# fabric preparation & cutting

*Wash, dry and press all quilting fabrics before you begin cutting. This ensures that the quilt will not shrink when it is laundered after you have sewn it.*

## cutting with a rotary cutter and ruler

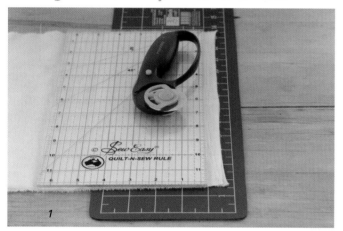

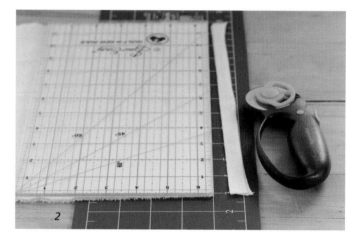

### step one

Lay the washed and pressed fabric on the cutting mat, aligning the grain with one of the grid lines on the mat. Place the quilting ruler over the top of the fabric, aligning it with the grid.

### step two

Slide the rotary cutter along the edge of the quilting ruler to cut through the fabric. You can cut through several layers of fabric at the same time. In this photograph, we have removed the selvedges of the fabric prior to cutting strips, squares or triangles for quilt blocks.

# cutting on the bias

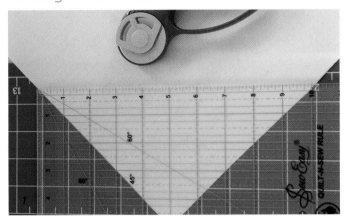

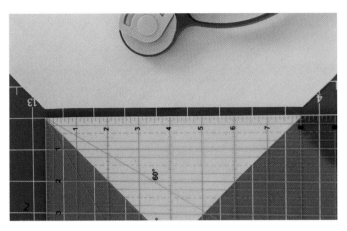

### step one

Remove the selvedges of a piece of fabric and ensure that the edges are cut straight along the warp and weft of the fabric. Place the fabric on the cutting mat. Align the 45 degree line on the quilting ruler with one edge of the fabric.

### step two

Slide the rotary cutter along the edge of the quilting ruler to cut through the fabric.

(If you do not have a 45 degree line on your ruler, fold the fabric so that the top edge aligns with the side edge and press the diagonal fold. Make your first cut along this fold.)

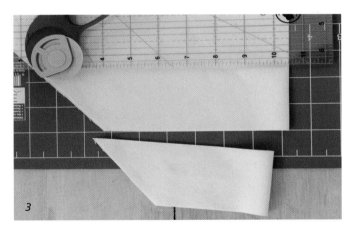

### step three

Cut strips of the desired width parallel to the first cut. In the photograph the strips are being cut 2½in (6.5cm) wide. Note that you can fold the fabric at right angles to the bias cut to allow you to cut longer bias strips. See page 125 for instructions on joining bias strips.

# patchwork techniques

*The basic methods of joining fabrics to make patchwork are illustrated on these pages.*

foundation piecing  *Using a paper pattern as a foundation, this method of patchwork is helpful when small pieces or sharp angles are included in a design. Foundation piecing is used in the queen-size bed quilt featured on page 20, and to create the zigzag pattern in the quilted cushion on page 48.*

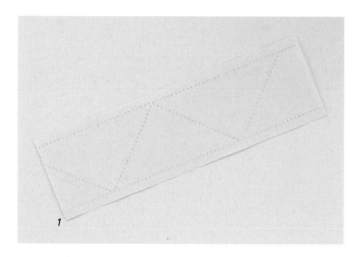

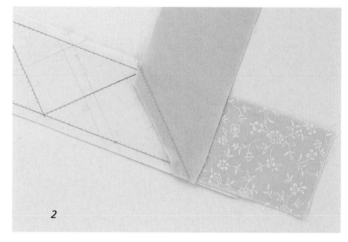

**step one**

Trace the pattern onto a piece of thin paper or tracing paper, ensuring that you include all seam allowances. With several sheets of paper together, stitch over the traced lines with an unthreaded sewing machine, to create additional copies of the pattern for multiple blocks in a quilt.

**step two**

Place a piece of fabric right-side up over the pattern, ensuring that the fabric covers the entire area of the first shape, including seam and cutting allowances. Place a second piece of fabric right-side down on top of the first.

Check that the second piece of fabric will completely cover the second shape on the pattern after it is stitched and turned right-side up. Pin the fabric in place, then turn the pattern over and stitch along the seam line through the paper and fabric.

crazy patchwork *This technique was developed as a way of recycling fabrics in the Victorian era, but it has found renewed popularity in recent years as a decorative alternative. The use of silks, satins and other glamour fabrics rather than quilting cottons is common. The quilted bolero on page 14 uses crazy patchwork.*

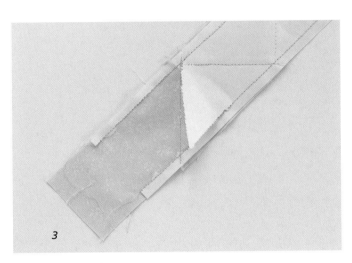

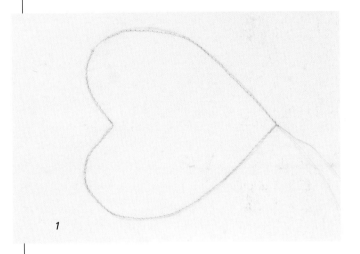

### step three

Trim the seam allowance to ¼in (6mm) without cutting the paper. Open the second fabric out. Press the fabric over the seam. Place a third piece of fabric as before, again ensuring that it will completely cover the third shape on the pattern. Stitch and trim the seam, then press the fabric over the seam. Continue placing fabric in this manner until the whole pattern has been covered. Trim the edges to the outer traced line of the pattern, then remove the paper. The perforations made by the machine needle will assist in tearing the pattern away.

### step one

Crazy patchwork can be used to cover blocks of any shape and size. Begin with a backing fabric and a shape to be patched. Machine stitch or baste by hand around the shape so that it is visible on both the right and wrong side of the fabric. This will ensure that you can still see the outline of the shape after it is completely covered by the patchwork fabrics.

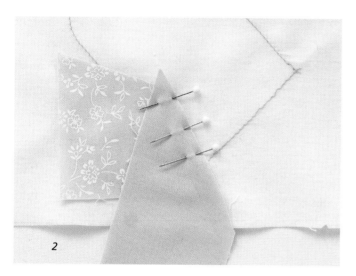

2

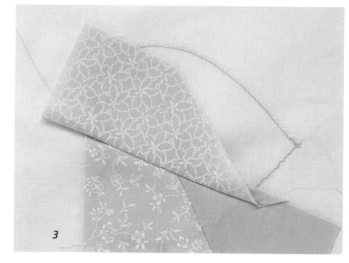

3

**step two**

Crazy patchwork is so-called because it does not use pieces of a specific shape and size, but irregular shapes that end up resembling the "crazed" effect of old porcelain. Cut an irregular shape, such as a lop-sided pentagon or trapezium and place it right-side up near the center of the backing fabric. Place a second fabric piece with right-side down on top of the first piece, with one edge aligned. Pin and stitch a ¼in (6mm) seam along the aligned edge, then open out the second fabric and press it over the seam.

**step three**

Place a third piece of fabric right-side down across one end of both of the previous pieces, aligning one edge of the new fabric roughly with the edges of the other two pieces. Pin and stitch as before, then trim the seam allowance carefully. Press the fabric open. Continue to add pieces of fabric until the entire shape is covered. Baste around the outline again to hold the edges of the crazy patchwork in place, then trim the entire block to the seam allowance around the original shape.

log cabin piecing *The log cabin block is a favourite basic patchwork block that is simply pieced with ¼in (6mm) seams. This block is the basis for the "Zigzag Pizzazz" quilted cushion on page 48.*

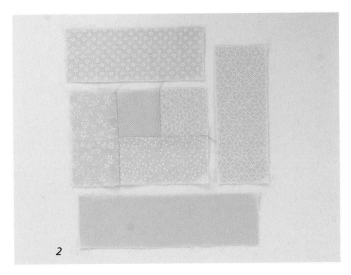

### step one

Begin with a square for the center of the block, in this case measuring 2½in (6.5cm). Traditionally, the center of a log cabin block is a plain red square, to represent the hearth at the heart of the cabin. Using a ¼in (6mm) seam, stitch another 2½in (6.5cm) square block to one side of the center block. Press the seam towards the center block.

Cut two more 2½in (6.5cm) wide strips of fabric to the length of the long edge of the center assembly. In this case, the strips are 4½in (11.5cm) long.

### step two

Attach one 2½in x 4½in (6.5cm x 11.5cm) strip to one long side of the center assembly. Press the seam towards the center of the block. Attach the remaining 2½in x 4½in (6.5cm x 11.5cm) strip to the end of the previous strip and the side of the center block, as shown in the photograph.

Cut two more 2½in (6.5cm) wide strips of fabric to the length of the long edge of the assembly. In this case, the strips are 6½in (16.5cm) long. Continue working clockwise around the center assembly, attaching pairs of strips until the block reaches the dimensions you desire.

# appliqué techniques

*There are two main forms of appliqué commonly used in quilting. Needleturn appliqué is the traditional method of blind stitching fabric shapes onto the quilt top. The recent invention of double-sided fusible interfacing has allowed the development of an easy alternative method.*

## fusible appliqué

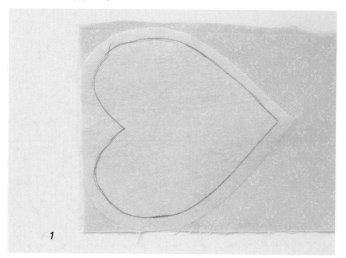

1

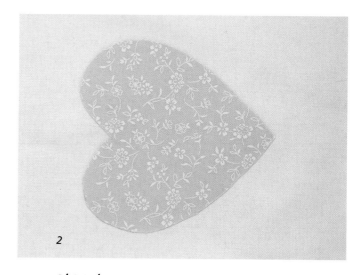

2

### step one

Draw or trace the appliqué shape onto the paper side of the double-sided fusible interfacing (also known as appliqué paper). Reverse the shape if it is not symmetrical. Cut the shape out roughly, about ¼in (6mm) from the traced line. Note that there is no hem allowance on fusible appliqué, as the fusing process prevents the edges from fraying.

Lay the fusible interfacing shape, paper side up, on the wrong side of the appliqué fabric. Following the manufacturer's instructions, press with an iron to fuse the interfacing to the fabric. Cut out the appliqué shape on the traced line.

### step two

Remove the paper backing, exposing the adhesive on the wrong side of the appliqué shape. Lay the shape right-side up, in position on the background fabric. Carefully press with an iron to fuse the two fabric layers together.

Complete the appliqué by stitching around the outer edge of the appliqué shape using blanket or buttonhole stitch. See page 128 for instructions on working this stitch.

## needleturn appliqué

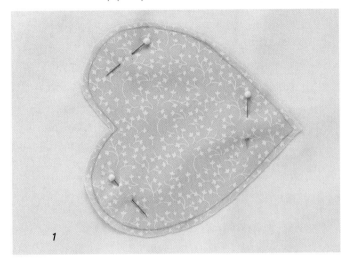

1

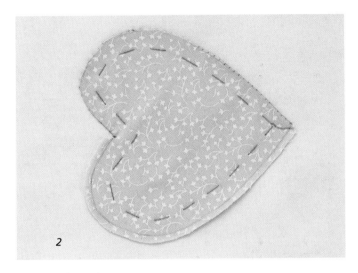

2

**step one**

Trace the appliqué shape onto the right side of the appliqué fabric, using a pencil or a temporary fabric marker. Cut out around the shape, ¹/₈in (3mm) from the traced line.

Lay the appliqué shape right-side up on the background fabric. Pin the shape in position. Baste the shape in place by stitching large running stitches ³/₈in (1cm) inside the traced line.

**step two**

Use sewing cotton to match the appliqué fabric and a betweens needle. (Darker sewing cotton has been used in the photograph for clarity.) Tuck the hem allowance under at the starting point of the stitching. Bring up the thread and needle from the wrong side of the background fabric. Pick up a couple of threads at the fold of the appliqué fabric, then take the needle and thread straight back through the background fabric. Take the needle and thread along ³/₁₆in (4mm) and bring them back to the front. Pick up a couple of threads of the appliqué fabric and take the needle and thread through the background fabric again. Continue stitching in this manner, turning the hem allowance as you go.

# quilting techniques

*The samples on these pages are designed to illustrate the basics of assembling, quilting and binding a quilt after the patchwork or decorative top is complete.*

## making a quilt sandwich

### step one

The backing fabric and batting are generally cut larger than the size of the finished quilt top. Lay the backing fabric, right-side down, on a flat surface and smooth it out. Use masking tape to temporarily hold it in place while you work. Lay the batting over the top of the backing fabric and smooth it out without stretching it.

### step two

Lay the finished and pressed quilt top over the batting and backing fabric. Smooth it out without stretching it. This completes the quilt "sandwich" of quilt top, batting and backing fabric. Pin the three layers of the sandwich together, ensuring the pins go all the way through to the backing fabric.

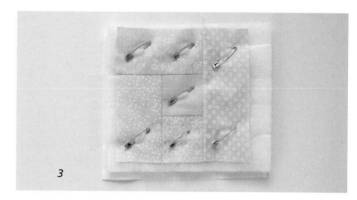

### step three

You can use quilting pins (steel pins with a long shaft) or safety pins. If you will be hand quilting, safety pins are preferable. For machine quilting, you will need to baste the layers together. Work a grid of long running stitches over the whole surface of the quilt, then remove the pins before machine quilting.

## hand quilting

## machine quilting

Hand quilting is worked with quilting thread or embroidery cotton and a betweens needle. With the quilt sandwich in a quilting hoop, make small running stitches (1/8in or 3mm long). Rock the needle back and forth through all the layers of fabric. Work only a few stitches at a time and keep the stitching even on both sides of the quilt.

Begin and end the threads by hiding the tails inside the quilt sandwich. Hand quilting is often worked as an echo of shapes and seams on the quilt top. The quilting is generally stitched 1/8–3/8in (3–10mm) from the feature that is being echoed.

Machine quilting is worked with quilting thread and a sewing or quilting machine. Straight stitches of a medium length can be worked on most sewing machines. This method lends itself to quilting in-the-ditch; that is, quilting along the seam lines of the quilt blocks and borders. In the photograph, the block has been quilted in-the-ditch and echo quilted as well.

Free machine quilting is possible on some domestic sewing machines. Using a specialised darning or quilting foot, with the feed dogs lowered, it is possible to manoeuvre the quilt sandwich so that the stitching flows in curves and free-form shapes over the surface of the quilt top. Stipple quilting (a filling stitch of randomly curved lines) is produced this way. A third method of machine quilting is to have the sandwich quilted by professional quilters using specialised quilting machines and, often, computerised stitching patterns. This is especially useful for really large quilts that won't easily feed through a domestic sewing machine.

## quilt-as-you-go

## tying a quilt

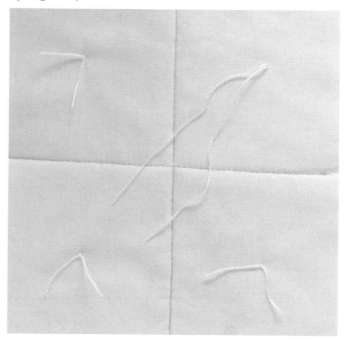

This quick and easy method involves making up small sandwiches of backing fabric, batting and top fabric for each quilt block, as shown above. Simply quilt the blocks as desired, such as with a straight machine stitch horizontally and vertically, before you assemble the quilt. Quilt-as-you-go quilts are often assembled with the seams on the front, so that the exposed seams become a feature of the quilt. Washing the quilt will cause the raw edges of the seams to fray softly and complete the casual look. The cot quilt on pages 58–61 uses this technique.

Another quick quilting method is tying. Using short lengths of embroidery thread or yarn, stitch through all layers of the quilt so that the ends of the threads are on the front of the quilt. Tie a secure knot in the thread ends and trim the threads about an inch from the knot. The knots and short ends of the threads become a feature of the quilt.

# binding a quilt

*Binding can be cut on the bias or on the straight grain of the fabric. You will usually need to join strips to make a length of binding sufficient for a quilt. Even if you cut the strips on the straight grain, use a bias seam to join them, as it reduces the bulk.*

### step one

Lay the strips at a 90 degree angle to each other. Pin and stitch a seam across the corner as shown in the photograph. Trim the seam allowance to no more than ¼in (6mm).

### step two

Open out the binding strip and press the seam open. Trim off excess seam allowance fabric to make a straight edge along the strip. Continue joining strips until you have a single strip of sufficient length to go all the way around the quilt.

### step three

Fold the binding strip in half lengthways, with wrong sides together. Press the fold to a sharp crease. Notice that the bias seam sits flatter than a straight seam, as the extra fabric in the seam allowance is spread over a larger area.

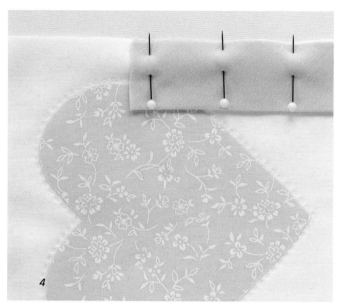

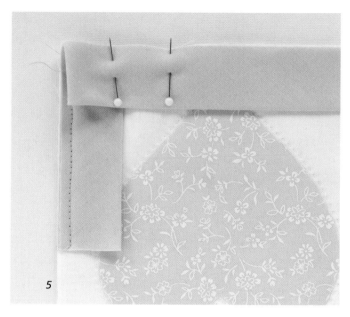

### step four

Beginning in the middle of one side edge of the quilt, pin the binding strip with its raw edges aligned with the raw edges of the quilt sandwich. Pin as far as the corner, then stitch the binding to the quilt through all layers, using a ¼in (6mm) seam.

Stop stitching ¼in (6mm) from the corner of the quilt. Remove the quilt from the sewing machine.

### step five

To mitre the corner, first fold the binding strip at a right angle to the sewn strip, away from the quilt. This will form a 45 degree fold at the corner. Holding this fold in place with your fingers, fold the binding strip at the edge of the quilt. This will bring the strip back onto the quilt, with the raw edges of the binding aligned with the raw edges of the quilt sandwich, as shown in the photograph.

6

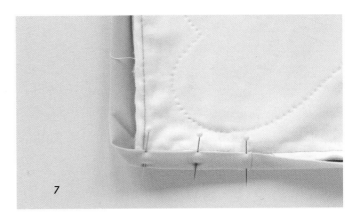

7

### step seven

Turn the folded edge of the binding strip over to the back of the quilt, aligning it with the stitching line. Pin the first side of the binding and stitch it to the quilt back with small slip stitches.

### step six

Stitch the binding to the quilt through all layers along this side, then repeat step five to mitre the corner. Continue all around the quilt, until you reach the beginning of the binding. Stop stitching at least 1in (2.5cm) from the starting point. Allow a short overlap of 1in (2.5cm) at both ends of the binding strip, and trim off the excess fabric.

Fold the raw edges of one end of the binding strip over by 3/8in (1cm) and slip this end over the raw edges of the other end. Finish sewing the binding strip to the quilt sandwich by sewing across the overlapped ends.

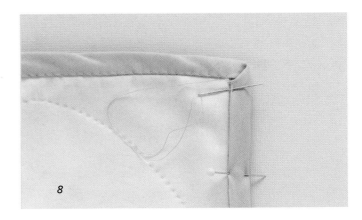

8

### step eight

Mitre the corner on the back of the quilt by allowing the binding to sit flat as in the photograph for step seven. When you have stitched up to the corner, fold the next side of the binding straight down, making a neat 45 degree fold at the corner on the reverse of the quilt as well as on the front. Continue slip stitching around all four sides of the quilt.

# stitches

*Some of the projects in this book use simple embroidery and hand-sewing stitches as well as quilting stitches.*

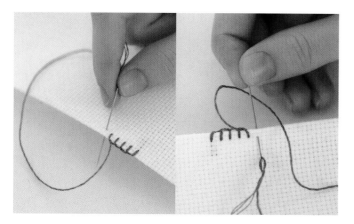

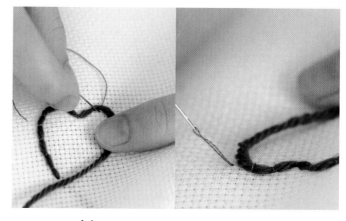

### buttonhole or blanket stitch

Buttonhole or blanket stitch is often used on the raw edges of fabric. In quilting, it is used for fusible appliqué. Starting with a knot on the wrong side of the fabric, bring the needle out at the edge of the fabric. Holding the loop of thread out of the way, place the needle back through the fabric at a point 1/8in (3mm) across and down from the starting point. The actual distance will depend on the desired size of your stitches, which can be as large as you like. Bring the needle to the front of the fabric at the raw edge. Ensure that it has passed through the loop of thread. Continue along the raw edges of the fabric in this manner until they are completely covered by the blanket stitching.

### couching

Couching is stitching with a fine thread to hold a thicker yarn or decorative fibre to the surface of the fabric. To begin, lay the thick yarn or fibre on the fabric in the desired shape. Pin it in place if you wish. Thread a needle with a single strand of embroidery or sewing thread in a matching color.

Take short stitches across the yarn or fibre, holding it to the fabric in the desired shape. Start and finish the embroidery thread on the wrong side of the fabric.

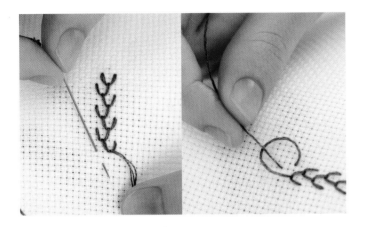

### feather stitch

Knot the end of the embroidery thread and bring the needle and thread up from the wrong side of the fabric. Holding the loop of thread below the stitch with your thumb, put the needle back into the fabric 1/8–1/4in (3–6mm) to one side of the point where the thread emerges. Bring the needle to the front of the fabric at a point making an equilateral triangle with the previous two points, inside the loop of thread. Pull the thread through to create a "U" shaped stitch. Holding the loop of thread below the stitch with your thumb, insert the needle 1/8–1/4in (3–6mm) from where the thread emerges, to the other side of the line of stitches. Bring the needle back up to make a triangle as before, inside the loop of thread. Continue alternating from left to right sides of the center line.

### herringbone stitch

Herringbone stitch is a variation of cross stitch, with long legs that cross over each other. Begin with a knot on the wrong side of the fabric. Bring the needle to the front of the fabric. Stitch diagonally across the area to be embroidered, making the stitch twice as long as the width. Take the needle back on the wrong side of the fabric half the distance to the original starting point, on the opposite side of the stitching. Make a second diagonal stitch back to the original side of the stitching. Take the needle back on the wrong side of the fabric and bring it to the front level with the opposite leg of the previous stitch. Continue stitching in the same manner.

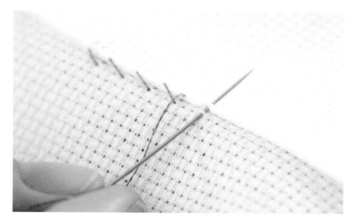

### ladder stitch

Ladder stitch is used to invisibly join two pieces of fabric, particularly to close openings left after turning items right-side out. It gets its name because the stitches look like the rungs of a ladder. Beginning with a knot between the two pieces of fabric, bring a needle threaded with sewing thread to the edge of the fold on one piece of fabric. Stitch across to the other piece of fabric, taking the needle for a short distance through the fold. Stitch back across to the first piece of fabric. Continue stitching in this manner until the opening is closed.

### slip stitch

Slip stitch is usually used for hemming or joining two pieces of fabric. It is sometimes called invisible hemming, because only the tiniest of stitches are visible on the right side of the fabric. Use sewing thread and begin with a knot hidden under the hem of the fabric. Bring the needle to the front of the hem, then take it along the hem for a short distance. Pick up a few threads from the main part of the fabric and pass the needle through the fold of the hem. Pull the stitch through, then take another stitch in the same way. Continue stitching until the hem is complete.

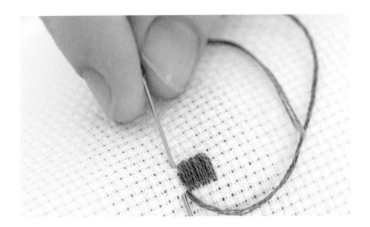

### satin stitch

This decorative stitch is a simple way of filling areas with color. Bring the needle and thread to the front of the fabric. Stitch across the area to be filled, and bring the needle up again next to the starting point. Keep the stitches close together, so that no fabric can be seen between them. When you have finished filling the area with color, take the needle and thread to the wrong side of the fabric. Work a small back stitch inside the back of the stitched area and pass the tail of the thread underneath the stitching to finish it off.

### stem stitch

Stem stitch gets its name because it is often used to embroider the stems of plants and flowers. Begin with a knot on the wrong side of the fabric. Bring the needle to the front and work a short stitch ($\frac{1}{8}$in or 4mm long, for example). Bring the needle up halfway along the stitch. (Hold the loop of thread out of the way as you stitch.) Pull the thread through, then work another stitch the same length as the first, this time bringing the needle up at the end of the first stitch. Continue in the same manner until the line of stitching is complete.

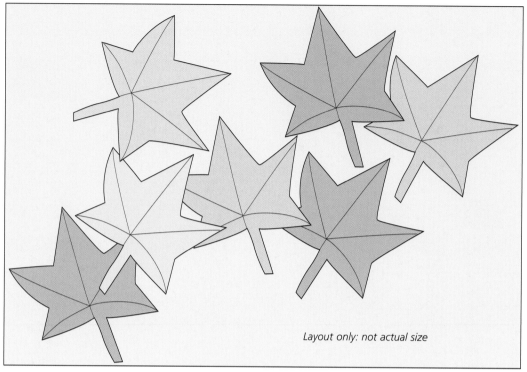

*Layout only: not actual size*

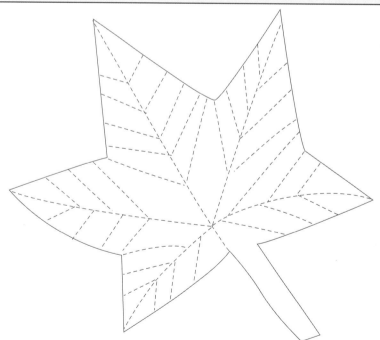

*Template at actual size*

*Template at 50% of actual size:
enlarge pattern 200%*

templates & patterns

133

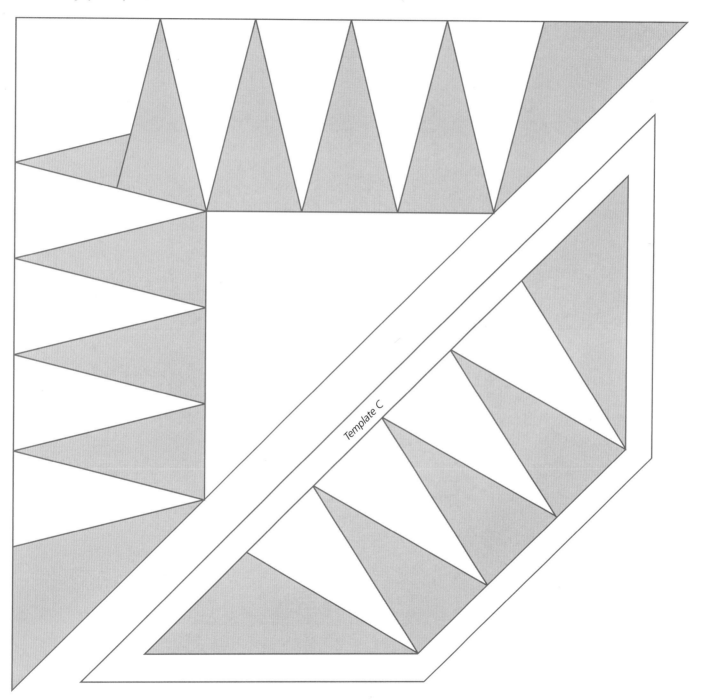

Template C

*Templates at actual size*

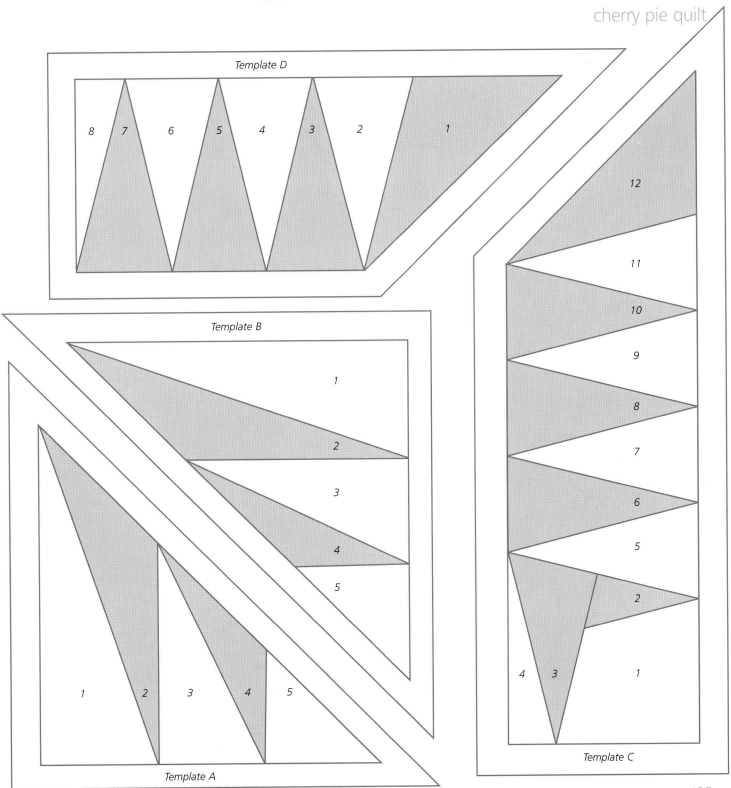

Template D

8  7  6  5  4  3  2  1

12

11

10

9

8

7

6

5

Template B

1

2

3

4

5

2

4  3  1

Template A

1  2  3  4  5

Template C

*Template at 40% of actual size:*
*enlarge pattern 250%*

*Template at 40% of actual size:*
*enlarge pattern 250%*

*Template at 50% of actual size:*
*enlarge pattern 200%*

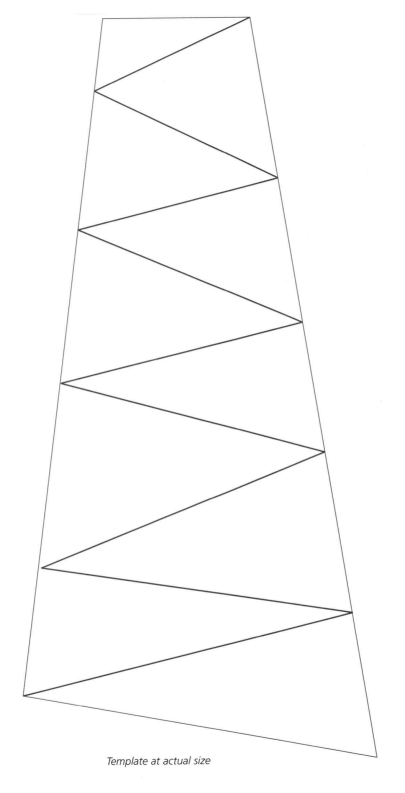

*Template at actual size*

*Template at 25% of actual size
enlarge pattern 400%*

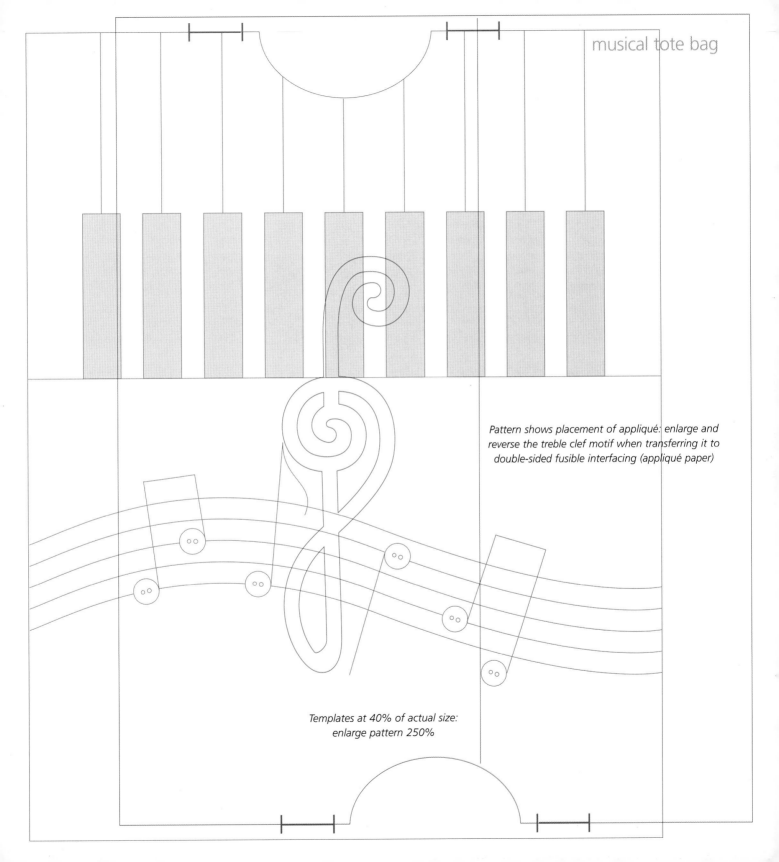

musical tote bag

Pattern shows placement of appliqué: enlarge and reverse the treble clef motif when transferring it to double-sided fusible interfacing (appliqué paper)

Templates at 40% of actual size: enlarge pattern 250%

# index

# index of artisans

# acknowledgements

Thank you to the following people and suppliers for their assistance with this book:

Heather and John Benbow

Humble Beginnings, Randwick, NSW

Meredith Kirton and Michael Bradford, Tess Bradford, Eden Bradford

Bronwyn Lear

Carla Mann

Alex Profilio

Lara Schilling

# inspirations books

*Editor*
Melody Lord

*Design and layout*
Susan Cadzow, Red Pepper Graphics

*Photography and styling*
Sue Stubbs

*Publisher*
Margie Bauer

Country Bumpkin Publications
315 Unley Road, Malvern
South Australia 5061
Phone: 08 8372 7600
Fax: 08 8372 7601
Email: marketing@countrybumpkin.com.au
Website: www.countrybumpkin.com.au

Published in Australia by Inspirations books
Printed and bound in the U.S.A.

Stitch it: Quilts
ISBN 978 09804359 1 7
COPYRIGHT © 2008 COUNTRY BUMPKIN PUBLICATIONS